COULD YOU LIVE UNDERWATER?

Grades 4-5

COULD YOU LIVE UNDERWATER?

A Design Thinking and STEM Curriculum Unit for Curious Learners

**Megan Barnhard
and Jade Rivera**

Routledge
Taylor & Francis Group

NEW YORK AND LONDON

First published in 2018 by Prufrock Press Inc.

Published in 2021 by Routledge
605 Third Avenue, New York, NY 10017
2 Park Square, Milton Park, Abingdon, Oxon OX14 4RN

Routledge is an imprint of the Taylor & Francis Group, an informa business.

Cover and layout design by Micah Benson

ISBN-13: 978-1-0321-4241-8 (hbk)
ISBN-13: 978-1-6182-1750-9 (pbk)

DOI: 10.4324/9781003233831

TABLE OF CONTENTS

INTRODUCTION

You are about to put some serious fun combined with deep learning into the hands of the bright learners you serve.

Here's what we know for sure: How people live and work is evolving rapidly and shows no signs of slowing. The way we connect, play, and learn looks wildly different from even 50 years ago. This new way of being requires both a quicker reaction time and a more complex thought process from our students—in school and beyond. Wouldn't it be great if there were a curriculum rooted in that reality that also imparted serious scientific knowledge while bolstering academic resiliency and risk-taking?

This STEM (science, technology, engineering, and math) curriculum for grades 4 and 5 teaches design thinking and valuable STEM skills via engaging projects that incorporate hands-on experimentation and building, research, active reading and analysis, writing, drawing, and creative reflection.

We wrote this book to help bring the best innovative thinking in successful 21st-century organizations into the hands of tomorrow's builders and leaders.

Design thinking is a way of thinking that successful creators use to build the processes and machines that enrich human life—from building the Mars rover to bringing fresh drinking water to remote locations. This thinking process is spreading to businesses and government institutions, becoming the new standard of innovation. Although it's great for building rockets, it's not rocket science. Any classroom can employ design thinking without a huge investment in technology or specialized equipment.

So, what is design thinking? As the name suggests, it's really just a way of thinking. It's a mental approach to solving problems that encourages collaboration, creativity, resilience, iteration, brainstorming, experimentation, reflection, and the celebration of small successes.

This design thinking curriculum proceeds as follows: After an engaging introduction module, there are six distinct modules to this unit, designed to walk your class through the tenets of design thinking as it relates to creating an undersea

 DOI: 10.4324/9781003233831-1

living space while addressing the complex issues of climate change and housing equity. Additionally, learners will explore the challenges that go along with making a life under the water at low temperatures and high pressure, with limited oxygen and other people in close quarters. The entire curriculum can be completed in six class periods, but it can also stretch to 6 weeks.

Students will love it because they get to design, build, and learn in a way that works for them. There will be a special appeal for kids interested in ecology and marine life. Creative thinkers and designers will get a kick out of inventing solutions to the problems of undersea living.

You will love it because you get to offer your students a real-world problem to solve while imparting the academic and critical thinking skills vital for success in an exciting and unpredictable future.

If those sound like traits you'd like to help build for your students, we think you'll really enjoy this curriculum.

So, let's dive in!

Introduction to Design Thinking

You may already know firsthand the power of problem-based learning. Students don't merely think; they do. They apply what they learn, and they build lasting knowledge.

This curriculum utilizes problem-based learning to engage learners. It also, however, teaches them to define the problem they will solve and to assess their success in solving it.

Design thinking invites thinkers to define problems to solve based on the human experience. Using empathy and connection, design thinking helps learners frame problems in terms of the effects on human beings—individuals, communities, and groups.

It also builds the habit of iteration. Learners become comfortable with "failing forward"—revisiting their ideas and modifying them not based on arbitrary designations of "good" or "bad" from an authority figure, but based on whether those ideas really worked to address a given problem! This kind of learning builds independence and curiosity as it invests power in learners, not letter grades.

The Five Stages of Design Thinking

Step 1: Empathize. Learners connect with people who are negatively impacted by a situation or condition. They come to understand the nuanced causes and wide-reaching effects of this condition.

Step 2: Define. Learners narrow their thinking and define one specific problem that they want to work on solving. This problem is born out of the empathy engendered in Step 1. Yet, it is also logically defined as a clear goal. For example, "We want to make life better for those affected by climate change" obviously springs from empathy. But it does not define a problem. On the other hand, this statement does: "We want to find new career opportunities for fishermen who have lost their livelihoods due to rising sea temperatures caused by climate change." Here, the problem is clearly defined: Fishermen have lost their ability to feed their families; they need new ways of earning a living.

Step 3: Ideate. In this stage, learners bring all of their ideas to the table. They explore and tap into their creativity. Using collaboration at this stage is especially powerful. Learners also conduct research so that their ideas are well thought out and grounded in background knowledge.

Step 4: Prototype or create. Learners build their designs as prototypes, returning as needed to the ideation process when materials in the real world don't behave quite as expected on paper. This key step brings their thinking into the world of materials and pushes learners to follow through on their ideas.

Step 5: Test. Learners test their prototypes based on specific and determined criteria. This stage is very powerful for learners as they experience a connection to practical outcomes. They'll know exactly what standards their projects need to meet. Further, they'll be able to observe for themselves whether their designs meet those standards! This is a very egalitarian mode of assessment. There is no limit to the number of designs that can be successful. There are not so many A's ready to be handed out; there is simply the reality-based judgment of what works. What about the designs that don't work? In design thinking, there are no failures; there are only iterations. Design thinking is recursive. The testing stage includes evaluating and taking notes about what could be done differently next time.

We've taken these design thinking elements as our foundation, and we've added two key pieces:

1. **Guided experimentation that enriches students' background knowledge of key science concepts.** Conducting these experiments firsthand will allow learners to connect with and understand the principles they'll be using in the design and prototype stages. Yes, they're going to have the opportunity to research and learn. But they will also get the excitement of seeing scientific inquiry in action! This is key for engaging learners in STEM topics and fueling their curiosity.

2. **Aspects of the writing process to help learners frame their thoughts, reflect on their experiences, and publish their findings.** At each stage of the design thinking process, learners will use brainstorming activities, writing frames, and journal prompts to put their experience into words. They will also "publish" their projects by creating Design Notebooks and sharing their designs via the web. Incorporating these writing elements builds a bridge between STEM topics and language arts, helping learners of all strengths and thinking styles find success.

How to Use This Book

Following an introductory module to introduce students to design thinking and set the stage for those classrooms that will be building a student blog, there are six distinct modules to this unit. Module 1: Empathizing and Setting Up the Problem begins with a personal note to learners from an invented character, which is intended to encourage imaginative thinking and intrinsic motivation. They learn how to define a problem based on what they read and learn about the real-world effects of climate change, specifically in relation to changing housing conditions.

The remaining modules guide students through the remaining three stages of design thinking: (1) research and ideation, (2) designing and building prototypes, and (3) testing prototypes. Between the research and designing stages, students also conduct experiments to increase their understanding of the properties of water. Following the final stage, learners share their findings and respond to the invented character from Module 1.

Each module includes objectives, an overview, a Tech Connection section with ideas for utilizing the web to share what students are doing, a Writing Connection section with ideas for enriching student learning through writing, mini-lessons, student handouts, and a Concluding Activities section with suggested journal entries, blog post titles, and other projects, where applicable.

Each module builds on those before it. Skipping modules or completing them out of order will create a disjointed and unsatisfying experience for students. The minimum amount of time needed to complete each module is 45 minutes.

As classes work through the modules, students will be creating records of their experience via their Design Notebooks. These binders hold students' designs, notes, worksheets, drafts, finished writing, and any supplemental work they create to document their design thinking journey. Students should be encouraged to personalize their Design Notebooks and to take pride in them.

 DOI: 10.4324/9781003233831-2

Suggested Time Frames

Although each module is important, the amount of time classrooms spend on each is flexible. Because the curriculum follows the stages of design thinking, it is far more important to utilize all of the modules in some way than to feel constrained about devoting a certain amount of time to each one.

The entire unit can be completed in six class periods, but it can also stretch to 6 weeks. Suggested time modifications are provided throughout in order to make this curriculum accessible to classrooms with a range of time, resources, and student size.

It is recommended that you begin each module by anchoring students in design thinking and reminding them of the purpose of the module. This can be a simple 30 seconds at the top of the lesson when the teacher or a student points to one of the created visual aids and says aloud which stage of design thinking the class is in. (These visual aids will be created during the Getting Started Module.)

The Getting Started Module is the most compact, requiring only a single class period of between 45 and 90 minutes.

The most in-depth module is Module 3, which introduces mini-lessons about the scientific process and a total of six experiments about the properties of water. Your classroom might choose to devote a week to Module 3 while only devoting single class periods to the other modules. On the other hand, your classroom might decide to use fewer of the experiments and complete Module 3 in one or two class periods.

Sample Time Frame

Each module includes an at-a-glance time frame chart. This allows you to determine which activities and mini-lessons to include for your class based on the time you have available for any given module.

Time Period	One Regular Period (45–90 min.)	One Extended Period (90–120 min.)	One Week (5 Class Periods)
Activities	• Research • Write • Define a problem	• Research • Write • Define a problem • Share	• Introduce the module • Research • Outline/draft • Revise • Define a problem • Share • Discuss/give feedback • Concluding Activities

One Class Period: The entire class works together researching by reading a single article. They work collaboratively to write a single-paragraph response as the teacher leads the process. Using this response, they then discuss and define a problem they will solve in the remaining modules.

One Extended Period: Students work in small groups, each group choosing a different article, creating its own short write-up (a single paragraph), and defining its own problem, which it then shares with the entire class.

One Week: Students work in groups or individually on articles of their choice; they write multi-paragraph responses to the articles they read, possibly even incorporating additional research they conduct in class via the Internet. After writing, each student or group defines the problem and then all students share with the class. Finally, students write about their experiences via journal entries and/or blog posts.

- **Day 1:** Select, read, and annotate articles.
- **Day 2:** Conduct additional research.
- **Day 3:** Outline and draft responses; consult with other groups/students. Brainstorm problem statements.
- **Day 4:** Revise and edit responses and problem statements.
- **Day 5:** Share and discuss responses and problem statements. Students take notes about the feedback they receive in order to build ideas for the next module. Students complete journal entries and/or blog posts.

Tech Connections

Although this unit doesn't rely on technology for its presentation and application, we have designed this unit with technology integrations in order to help students share their work and also practice effective digital habits. Although optional, the tech connection component of each module has several benefits, as follows.

This unit of study has themes of iteration and graduated growth at its core. If students have an avenue for publishing their work, they will have an intrinsic motivation to give their best effort. Sharing work outside the boundaries of the classroom lends a feeling of seriousness to what students are doing and encourages them to push themselves so that each new draft or iteration of the project becomes something of which they will be proud. Sharing the project online is an accessible and inexpensive way for students to achieve the benefits of publishing in a public sphere.

Additionally, publishing their work online via social media and using hashtags will allow students to make real-world connections with professionals in the STEM fields they are exploring in this unit. They will have a taste of what it is like to operate within the scientific community and hopefully become inspired to continue and grow the connections they make. Students will be more likely to see the value in what they do in the classroom—and thus invest in their learning—when they see the possibility of engaging with real-world problem solvers and issues.

Finally, the suggested tech connections will help students build healthy Internet habits and social-emotional skills by interacting with others. A lot of emphasis is placed on what not to do online for younger students. We see great value in helping upper elementary students learn what they *can* do, thereby empowering them to become productive and responsible Internet users and social media participants. Students will be able to apply the concepts of empathy they are learning in this unit to their interactions with others as they navigate the online space.

Tech connections can be made in a number of ways. We highly recommend avenues that allow the entire class to participate together. This includes, but isn't limited to, a classroom Twitter account, a classroom Instagram account, a classroom Facebook page, and a classroom blog on a free blogging platform. (See Appendix B for suggested platforms and resources for adding images to blog posts.) Using the hashtag #couldyouliveunderwater will enable your students to see what other classrooms are doing with this unit of study, further exciting and inspiring them.

At the end of each module, you will find specific suggestions for utilizing the tech connections, including ideas for blog and social media posts.

Writing Connections

There are plenty of opportunities for students to utilize and hone their writing skills as they summarize and reflect on their learning. Each module has suggestions for journal entries that students can complete and add to their Design Notebooks. These informal responses allow students to reflect on their feelings, learning, and triumphs and challenges within a module.

Following each module, you will also find suggested blog titles. For classrooms maintaining a blog to document and enhance this unit, the blog posts are opportunities for students to practice more polished writing that will be published. The suggested titles are intended to point students in helpful directions and spark their thinking, but, of course, they can invent their own blog post topics and titles. Your students might use the suggested titles as templates, personalizing common blog title structures to fit their unique ideas.

Some modules contain more formal writing projects, such as essays, reports, or letters. When these appear, you will find student handouts with frames and/or outlines so that students have some parameters for structuring their thoughts. These writing templates can be switched out for outlines and processes that your class uses regularly or that you know are successful for your students.

We highly recommend that students share their writing with their peers for feedback and inspiration, as well as to encourage them to put their best work forward, knowing others will read it. To that end, we have included material for guiding your students through the process of offering feedback. In Module 1, you'll find Mini-Lesson 1.5: What Should I Say?: A Guide to Effective Feedback. The skills from this mini-lesson can be used throughout the entire unit to help students provide one another with constructive criticism.

MATERIALS

All modules require Design Notebooks for students to use for the duration of the project. These should be one-inch three-ring binders (one for each learner) with dividers for each module (six for each learner). The Design Notebooks allow students to compile writing and drawings that they complete over the course of the unit. The Design Notebooks begin empty except for the dividers. Students will fill and construct their Design Notebooks throughout the unit, eventually creating tables of contents for them in Module 6.

Having binders that students fill with their work allows students to hand-write neatly or type, depending on the needs of their classroom, and all papers can simply be hole-punched and added to the correct section of the binder. The last module provides time and instruction for students to gather and organize all of the materials they have created into their Design Notebooks. Whether students transport their Design Notebooks back and forth between school and home, or whether they leave them in the classroom and complete any assignments on binder paper, is up to you.

Each mini-lesson includes a list of suggested materials, including student handouts and other resources. Some specific materials related to the modules are described in this section in more detail.

Getting Started Module

The Getting Started Module requires materials for creating posters or infographics about design thinking, such as unlined paper or poster paper, as well as crayons, markers, or other art supplies.

You will need to create an example visual aid of the design thinking process, as outlined in the Getting Started Module, to present to students. Before teaching this lesson, you will need to go through the module on your own and make the visual aid described.

Module 2

Module 2 requires research materials about the ocean that focus on pressure, density, temperature, and impact on man-made materials and on potential dangers to humans, such as predatory animals, extreme conditions, or toxic elements. These might be articles found online or books checked out from the school or local library. There are a few articles listed on Handout 2.5 to get you started.

Module 3

Module 3 features six unique experiments. The materials and instructions for each are included on the handouts in this module (see pp. 82–93).

Module 4

Module 4 has students begin building their prototype underwater habitats. Classrooms may gather whatever supplies they like for building prototypes. This is a great time to engage learners' families and ask what kinds of materials they may be able to supply at low cost or for free. When choosing what materials to bring into your classroom for the building portions of this book, do not over-think things. A random scattering of household items and what you normally might recycle are ideal for prototyping and building the underwater habitats. The goal should be for all students to have access to the same materials. Designs will vary from student to student, but you can get students thinking in the right direction by encouraging them to include the following elements:

- a frame,
- a covering that contains the frame, and
- a waterproofing element.

Here are some suggested building materials:
- Duct tape
- Cardboard
- Used recyclables (such as cleaned milk cartons, toilet paper roll tubes, paper towel tubes, paper and plastic shopping bags, etc.)
- Cardstock
- Masking tape
- Electrical tape
- Aluminum foil
- Plastic cling wrap
- Pipe cleaners
- Twist ties
- Paraffin wax (the kind commonly given to orthodontia patients)
- PVC pipe (cut into 6- to 8-inch lengths)
- Hot glue gun (and glue sticks)
- Brads
- Tacks
- Glue sticks
- Stapler (and staples)

Module 5

Module 5 requires students to test their prototypes. You will need a clear plastic storage container (32–40 liters in size), water to fill the container, and salt to approximate the ocean's salinity (around 3.5%) in the testing container of water. Use approximately 35 grams of salt per liter of water.

Module 6

In Module 6, students will need pens, markers, crayons, paints, etc., to create final presentations of their projects and to finish their Design Notebooks.

MEETING STANDARDS

This unit is designed to be adapted for use within a variety of classroom settings. Thus, the standards it addresses will vary based upon an individual classroom's needs and how the instructor chooses to implement the unit.

By its very nature, however, this unit meets Next Generation Science Standards (NGSS) for grades 3–5 in engineering and design. The core of the unit asks students to conduct research and analyze the ways in which they can use scientific thinking to protect the Earth's resources and environment. Their main activity will be to define a simple design problem that reflects a need and that includes specific criteria for success and constraints on materials and time.

Furthermore, this unit meets several Common Core State Standards (CCSS) for English Language Arts for grades 4–5 when classrooms utilize the included writing projects and suggested assignments, including the upkeep of a classroom blog.

To see specific standards addressed, the end of the unit includes a CCSS alignment chart and an NGSS alignment chart.

ASSESSMENT

Throughout the unit there will be an opportunity to utilize specialized assessment rubrics that help you evaluate your students based on core skills they are learning, not only related to STEM and writing topics, but also to social-emotional skills, such as collaboration and working with purpose. Each of the following rubric descriptions includes recommendations about where and how to use each rubric. The rubrics are included in Appendix C.

Writing Assessment Rubric

Recommended for use with Modules 1, 2, 6, and any modules for which students complete writing assignments in the Concluding Activities section. Use this rubric to evaluate students' completed writing for this unit. The maximum number of points is 100 (20 points for each of the five categories). Points should be awarded between 0 and 20 as you see fit.

Hands-On Activity Assessment Rubric

Recommended for use with Modules 3,4, and 5. Use this rubric to evaluate students' work on the guided experiments as well as on designing and testing their prototypes. The maximum number of points is 100 (20 points for each of the five categories). Points should be awarded between 0 and 20 as you see fit.

Design Notebook Assessment Rubric

Recommended for use with Module 6. Use this rubric to evaluate students' completed Design Notebooks. The maximum number of points is 100 (20 points for each of the five categories). Points should be awarded between 0 and 20 as you see fit.

Other Forms of Assessment

Students will also have the chance to evaluate one another's work. In the Getting Started module, Module 1, and Module 5, they will use rubrics, handouts, or the instructions provided in mini-lessons to provide peer assessment. These should be seen as opportunities to help set a positive tone of collaboration and fair-minded evaluation among your students.

Students will also have the chance to self-evaluate in this unit. Module 4 includes a Self-Evaluation Handout (Handout 4.5) that helps students think critically about the success of their prototypes. In addition, each module includes journal prompts that encourage students to reflect on their performance during the activities. You might choose to utilize these as part of the assessment process so that students have a hand in evaluating their own performance throughout the unit.

SHARING STUDENT WORK

We highly recommend displaying student work from the outset of this unit. Share it proudly in the classroom and beyond. Within the classroom, consider displaying the posters students create about design thinking, as well as their drawings of designs, their responses to the articles they read in Module 1, and any other work produced that is inspiring, or of which students are particularly proud.

Photos and videos of student work and the writing they complete to reflect on the project in the Concluding Activities of each module can be shared online via a class blog or social media accounts. For specific suggestions, make sure to consult the Tech Connections section of each module. If you would like to set up a classroom blog where your class can share updates and progress throughout the entire unit, check out Mini-Lesson 0.2 about making a classroom blog in the Getting Started Module.

At the conclusion of this unit, provide students with an opportunity to share their completed Design Notebooks with their community. This might mean inviting faculty, parents, or other classes into your classroom for a tour of the Design Notebooks and the materials displayed on the walls and for a viewing of the student presentations from Module 6. It might also mean filming and photographing the Design Notebooks and the final presentations to share on the classroom blog or social media accounts. Find creative ways for your students to share their work. Each opportunity to describe what they have done in this unit deepens students' connection to their work and solidifies their retention of the design thinking process.

WHAT IS DESIGN THINKING?

Objectives

In this module, students will demonstrate their understanding of design thinking via visual presentations of its five stages. Students will also use a rubric to assess their peers in order to build critical thinking skills and empathy.

Overview

The teacher will introduce the class to the tenets of design thinking in a relatable way, calling upon students' past experience.

Tech Connections

Photograph or film students' posters for the classroom Facebook page, Instagram page, Twitter account, and/or blog. Use the hashtag #couldyouliveunderwater.

Writing Connections

This module includes a mini-lesson about how to write a blog post for classrooms interested in setting up classroom blogs. There are suggested blog posts in the Concluding Activities section for those classrooms keeping a blog. Encourage students to use the provided blog post titles as inspiration for what they will write.

15   DOI: 10.4324/9781003233831-3

Time Frame

Time Period	One Regular Period (45–90 min.)	One Extended Period (90–120 min.)
Activities	• Mini-Lesson 0.1: What Does Design Thinking Have to Do With Me? • Create and present design thinking posters • Peer assessment of design thinking posters utilizing Handout 0.2: Poster Assessment Rubric	• Mini-Lesson 0.1: What Does Design Thinking Have to Do With Me? • Create and present design thinking posters • Peer assessment of design thinking posters utilizing Handout 0.2 Poster Assessment Rubric • Mini-Lesson 0.2: Introduction to Blogging

One Class Period: The teacher presents his or her poster about design thinking. Students work in small groups to read and discuss Handout 0.1: What Does Design Thinking Have to Do With Me? Students or groups of students then create their own posters outlining the tenets of design thinking and evaluate their peers using Handout 0.2: Poster Assessment Rubric.

One Extended Period: The teacher presents his or her poster about design thinking. Students work in small groups to read and discuss Handout 0.1: What Does Design Thinking Have to Do With Me? Students or groups of students then create their own posters outlining the tenets of design thinking and evaluate their peers using Handout 0.2: Poster Assessment Rubric. The teacher guides the class through Mini-Lesson 0.2: Introduction to Blogging. A blog schedule is created, assigning different students different modules.

WHAT DOES DESIGN THINKING HAVE TO DO WITH ME?

Suggested Materials

- Teacher's design thinking poster
- Unlined paper or poster paper (for creating infographics or posters about design thinking)
- Crayons, markers, or other art supplies
- Student copies of Handout 0.1: What Does Design Thinking Have to Do With Me?

Teacher's Note. Prior to this mini-lesson, complete these activities on your own to become comfortable with the process and mindset necessary for a successful design thinking experience. Create your own design thinking poster to use as a visual when you present the concepts to your students.

Sequence

1. Tell students that they're going to be using an approach called *design thinking.* Ask students to share any prior knowledge they have about design thinking. Tapping into the wisdom of your classroom will set the stage for autonomous thought and problem solving.

2. After a short discussion, present your poster to your students and explain that you've been learning about design thinking and are excited to share this method of learning with them.

3. Divide students into small groups (this can also be done individually), and distribute Handout 0.1: What Does Design Thinking Have to Do With Me? for students to read as a group. Circulate to help keep students on task and assist as needed. After 10 minutes, bring the class back together for a discussion.

4. Share with students the stages of design thinking by referencing your own poster. Show them the sequence and the process that they will be using over the course of the unit.

5. After a short discussion, reviewing the highlights of the handout, reintroduce each element of design thinking. Ask students questions about each step as a means of brainstorming ideas for students' (or groups') infographics or posters. (Suggested questions are included for each stage of design thinking.)

6. **Step 1. Empathize:** Explain to students that the first step of the design thinking process requires them to listen/observe, ask questions in order to understand, feel what other people are feeling (put themselves in others' shoes), and assume that others are trying their best. In other words, it requires them to *be empathetic*. Possible questions for discussion include:

   o When have you empathized with someone?
   o What is challenging about empathizing? Have you ever had a hard time understanding where someone else was coming from (i.e., a friend, sibling, or adult)?
   o What does it feel like to help someone who needs your help?
   o What does it feel like to get help when you need it?

7. **Step 2. Define:** Students need to determine what the problem is, why it occurs, how it affects people, what it would take to solve it, and what the solved scenario would look like. Possible questions for discussion include:

   o What are some problems we have had in our classroom? (Paintbrushes getting dried out with paint on them and being ruined? Not enough paper? A long line for the water fountain at recess? Invite students to think of concrete problems they've encountered.)
   o Why are these things problems? How do they affect us?
   o What does it feel like when these problems arise?
   o Do these problems lead to other problems?

8. **Step 3. Ideate:** Step 3 requires students to brainstorm, brain-dump, mind-map, talk it out, collaborate with others to get all of the best ideas they can, and build off of other people's ideas to develop and refine them. Possible questions for discussion include:

   o How did we solve those problems from Step 2?
   o If we haven't solved them, how could we? (Model a brainstorming process by writing down all of the possible ideas students have and asking them to build on the ideas of other students. For example, if one student says that the class should make a rule about always washing out paintbrushes right after they're used, you could ask the rest of the class how to make this happen. Other students might suggest putting a sign up by the sink to remind everyone or wrapping up art projects a few minutes earlier so that there is time to clean up properly.)

9. **Step 4. Prototype:** Explain that students will be building the idea from Step 3 out of expendable materials. If building isn't an option, share a sketch of the design on paper. Students should remember to be flexible. (Is there a different material they could use? What problems arise that

they didn't foresee? Creating a prototype is like sketching the idea in 3-D or creating a rough draft. It will not be a beautiful, finished product, and that's just fine!) Possible questions for discussion include:

o   Why do you think making a prototype is important?

o   Let's think about the Mars rover. Why would NASA want to build a prototype of the rover on Earth before sending it to Mars? What are the kinds of tests NASA would want to run on the prototype?

o   What problems might arise if we didn't prototype our ideas before people used them?

o   Can we think of any examples of inventions in our world right now that are being prototyped (e.g., self-driving cars)? What would happen if they weren't tested first?

10. **Step 5. Test:** Students need to determine their testing criteria, use qualitative and quantitative evaluation, and observe, observe, observe! While testing, students should track their observations and write down their conclusions. Possible questions for discussion include:

o   How could we test whether our solutions in Step 3 worked? What would our criteria be?

o   What do you think we would do if our solutions didn't work? What do you think the next step might be after Step 5? (Students should understand that returning to Step 3 or Step 4 would be helpful.)

o   What are your experiences of having to try more than once to do something? Tying your shoes? Riding a bike, skateboard, or scooter? Playing an instrument?

INTRODUCTION TO BLOGGING

Suggested Materials

- Classroom computer, laptop, or tablet with Internet access
- Projector and any necessary connecting cables to project from the laptop or tablet
- URLs of 2–3 sample blog posts to show the class (look for posts that inspire and inform)

Teacher's Note. Prior to this mini-lesson, locate two or three blog posts that are age-appropriate and of interest to your class so that you can present them as examples. These might be posts from science or engineering blogs published by adults, or they might be posts from classroom or student blogs.

Sequence

1. Tell students that they're going to be using a blog to share their design thinking experiences with the general public. Ask: *What do you know about blogs? What are they for? Who creates them? Who reads them?*

2. After a short discussion, tell students that the purpose of their classroom blog will be to inform and inspire others who are interested in design thinking. Using the projector or simply the computer if all students are able to see the screen, show the first blog post. Read it aloud while scrolling through it. Ask students to give their opinion of its purpose: *Does it inspire, inform, or both?* Work through each example in this way.

3. Next, demonstrate the format of an engaging blog post. Show students that each post has a descriptive title and a featured image. Point out the use of elements that make the material highly readable, including headers, images, and video.

4. Finally, decide as a class how frequently you will add new posts to the classroom blog and make a blogging calendar so that each student knows when he or she will be responsible for writing a post. Let students know that you will be offering them suggestions of what to blog about for each module.

Teacher's Note. Appendix B has helpful links to some free blogging platforms, as well as to tools for creating blog graphics.

CONCLUDING ACTIVITIES

Suggested Assignment

Individually, in pairs, or in small groups, have students create posters/infographics outlining the steps of the design thinking process, including examples from history, the current world, or their own experiences. Students will present their posters to the class and then use Handout 0.2: Poster Assessment Rubric to evaluate the posters for (a) clear communication, (b) audience engagement, and (c) relevancy. Hang the posters around the classroom for the duration of this project to act as a reminder that design thinking is a circular process that requires an open mind and resilience.

Suggested Blog Posts

- What Is Design Thinking?
- Are You Already Using Design Thinking in Your Everyday Life?
- 5 Ways To Think Like a Designer
- 10 Inventions That Wouldn't Exist Without Design Thinking
- 5 Tips for Making a Memorable Poster

Handout 0.1

What Does Design Thinking Have to Do With Me?

Design thinking is the art of gaining knowledge or understanding about a specific problem with the hope of improving that knowledge and understanding while ultimately solving that problem. *Design thinking* is also an esoteric term for an action that you've been taking your entire life—learning.

As a baby, you were born with very few communication skills, but you were presented with the problem of getting what you need. You tried out cries, the use of your body, gestures, and babbling before you stumbled upon a strategy that worked for you. Then, you improved and expanded upon that strategy. As a natural communicator, you learned through trial and error how to become a better communicator. We're never done learning how to communicate. We're only getting better.

The process that you underwent as a newborn is nearly identical to the process used to solve many of the complex challenges we face today:

- First, you empathized with a real-world problem. Empathy for yourself counts! You really wanted to communicate your needs to those around you. It was literally a matter of life and death.
- Then, you defined your problem. "I need a way to get the things I need from others." It probably wasn't as conscious a thought as that, but you defined the problem nonetheless!
- You researched by observing how others were communicating around you.
- You created (designed) a way of communicating that worked for you.
- Next, you tested out this new way of communicating on those around you.
- Lastly, you iterated and evaluated what worked and what didn't about your previous communication efforts in the hope of communicating more effectively in the future.

Design thinking is nothing more than a loose framework for learning. The constraints of empathizing, researching, creating, testing, evaluating, and iterating only serve to create a path of learning and problem solving. It's common for those new to design thinking to apply these steps with rigidity while not taking into account that ultimately this is a creative endeavor. Try to think of design thinking as a circular process rather than a linear one and you're on your way!

Now that you know what design thinking is, how many other times have you used this framework to solve a problem or learn something new?

Name: _____ Date: _____

Handout 0.2
Poster Assessment Rubric

Directions: Use this rubric to evaluate the posters made by your classmates. The maximum number of points is 100 (20 points for each of the five categories). Points should be awarded between 0 and 10 and between 10 and 20 as you see fit.

Name:

	0 points	10 points	20 points
Title	No title on poster.	Title is unclear on poster and is unrelated to poster information.	Title is clear and related to poster information.
Tenets of Design Thinking	Poster does not include the tenets of design thinking.	Poster is missing some tenets and/or the tenets are out of order.	Poster contains each tenet of design thinking in the correct order.
Relevant Example	Poster does not include an example.	The example is not relevant to the design thinking process.	Poster includes a relevant example of how design thinking is used in real life.
Writing and Grammar	Writing is absent from poster.	Writing and grammar used on the poster was not proofread and revised. Words are spelled incorrectly.	Writing and grammar used on the poster has been proofread and revised.
Appearance	It appears that no effort was made to create an attractive poster.	Some effort was made to create an attractive poster.	The poster is attractive and engaging to look at.

Notes:

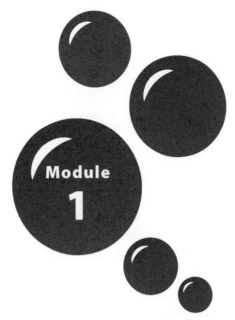

EMPATHIZING AND SETTING UP THE PROBLEM

Objectives

In this module, students will actively read and recall nonfiction text; effectively manage information; explore and develop individualized annotation skills; process and respond to a problem using empathy; plan and write responses to material they have read using writing templates; and define a problem clearly and concisely using writing frames and a checklist.

Overview

Students will complete empathy-building exercises in order to gain a critical and compassionate understanding of a real-world situation in order to define a problem in relation to people. In order to define the problem they will be solving, students will learn about the impacts of a pressing global problem: a changing climate. They will research how global climate change is affecting nations, communities, and families.

Students read a letter written to them that communicates the important personal attributes necessary for getting the most out of the subsequent modules, namely, creativity, resilience, and commitment. This can be done individually, as a class, or in groups. Teachers are encouraged to get as theatrical as they like with this, and even bring in a person from the community to deliver the letter.

Students read articles about nations, communities, and families affected by climate change. They actively read and respond to the material for improved

 DOI: 10.4324/9781003233831-4

understanding. Students then write responses to the articles they read. These responses summarize the events and clearly identify a problem that they, the students, would like to focus on solving. Once they have written their responses to the problem, students define the problem they will be solving using Handout 1.8: Tools for Defining the Problem.

Tech Connections

Students can write and publish posts on the classroom blog. (See "Suggested Blog Posts" in the Concluding Activities section.) The problem statements created using Handout 1.8 can be tweeted on the classroom Twitter account, using the hashtag #couldyouliveunderwater. Student problem statements can also be photographed, or students can be recorded reading their problem statements, and these can be shared on Instagram with that same hashtag.

Writing Connections

Students will be writing responses to the article(s) they read. These responses can be a few sentences, a significant paragraph, or multi-paragraph essays. Choose the length of writing that best matches the time available and the skill level of your students. Templates for all three lengths of response are provided as individual handouts (Handouts 1.4–1.6), so you can also mix and match what your students are doing in order to ensure success for all while providing the appropriate level of challenge. All students can benefit from using Handout 1.7: Transition Words and Phrases to add clarity and flow to their writing. You will also find helpful templates for building problem statements in Handout 1.8: Tools for Defining the Problem. This handout shows sample problem statements and includes a checklist and writing frames to help students build their own effective problem statements following design thinking guidelines.

There are also suggested journal entries and suggested blog posts in the Concluding Activities section. For classrooms keeping a blog, encourage students to use the provided blog post titles as inspiration for what they will write.

Time Frame

Time Period	One Class Period (45–90 min.)	One Extended Period (90–120 min.)	One Week (5 Class Periods)
Activities	• Mini-Lesson 1.1: Introducing the Problem • Read selected articles	• Mini-Lesson 1.1: Introducing the Problem • Mini-Lesson 1.2: What Should I Highlight? • Read selected articles	• Mini-Lesson 1.1: Introducing the Problem • Mini-Lesson 1.2: What Should I Highlight? • Read selected articles

Time Period, *continued.*	One Class Period (45–90 min.), *continued.*	One Extended Period (90–120 min.), *continued.*	One Week (5 Class Periods), *continued.*
Activities, *continued.*	• Mini-Lesson 1.3: How Would That Feel?: A Guide to Building Empathy • Collaboratively write responses using Student Response Templates (Handout 1.4 or Handout 1.5, plus Handout 1.7, if time permits) • Collaboratively create a problem statement using Handout 1.8: Tools for Defining the Problem	• Mini-Lesson 1.3: How Would That Feel?: A Guide to Building Empathy • Write responses using Student Response Templates (Handout 1.4 or Handout 1.5, plus Handout 1.7) • Create a problem statement using Handout 1.8: Tools for Defining the Problem	• Mini-Lesson 1.3: How Would That Feel:? A Guide to Building Empathy • Outline/draft responses using Student Response Templates (Handouts 1.6 and 1.7) • Revise/edit responses • Create a problem statement using Handout 1.8: Tools for Defining the Problem • Mini-Lesson 1.5: What Should I Say?: A Guide to Effective Feedback • Share/discuss problem statements • Concluding Activities

One Class Period: The teacher shares the letter (Handout 1.1) with the class. The class works together as a group on a single article, a single write-up (a single paragraph that they write collaboratively with the teacher guiding), and defining a single problem.

One Extended Period: The teacher shares the letter (Handout 1.1) with the class. Students work in small groups, each group choosing a different article, creating its own short write-up (a single paragraph), and defining its own problem, which it then shares with the entire class.

One Week: The teacher shares the letter (Handout 1.1) with the class. Students work in groups or individually on articles of their choice; they write multi-paragraph responses to the articles they read, possibly even incorporating additional research they conduct in class via the Internet. After writing, each student or group defines the problem, and then all students share with the class for feedback.

- **Day 1:** Read letter. Select, read, and annotate articles.
- **Day 2:** Conduct additional research.
- **Day 3:** Outline and draft responses; consult with other groups/students. Brainstorm problem statements.
- **Day 4:** Revise and edit responses and problem statements.
- **Day 5:** Share and discuss responses and problem statements. Students take notes about the feedback they receive in order to build ideas for the next module. Students work on journal responses and/or blog posts.

Mini-Lesson 1.1

INTRODUCING THE PROBLEM

Suggested Materials

- Student Design Notebooks
- Student copies of Handout 1.1: Welcome Letter

Sequence

1. Explain to students that they are beginning their design thinking journey by empathizing with people and places that have been affected by the effects of climate change on housing.
2. Ask students to share what they already know about climate change and how it is already affecting people and housing. You may want to warn students that some of the research they will read in this module may be upsetting. Set aside time for processing students' feelings about what they learn. Reiterate that they have the power to have a positive impact on this problem, and that is why participating in projects like this is so important.
3. Distribute Handout 1.1: Welcome Letter to students, along with the binders in which they will build their Design Notebooks. Introducing the letter could be as straightforward as reading it aloud as a class, or it could be as elaborate as having a guest come to class in character as Mariana Trench Sandoval to deliver the message live.

Mini-Lesson 1.2

WHAT SHOULD I HIGHLIGHT?: A GUIDE TO ACTIVE READING AND ANNOTATING

Suggested Materials

- Teacher's copy of a well-known story that allows students to see examples of the 5 W's and 1 H
- Student Design Notebooks
- Student copies of Handout 1.2: What Should I Highlight?: A Guide to Active Reading and Annotating

Sequence

1. Let students know they're about to jump into some serious research so that they can start solving the problem of how to design an underwater habitat. Because they will get a lot of interesting and important information, they will want to have a strategy in place for sifting through all of that information and determining what is the most important.

2. Tell students: *The reason we highlight is so that we don't have to reread the entire text when we want to remember what it contained. Th s, helpful highlighting picks out a small number of critically important words and phrases to jog our memories without overloading our eyes. Highlighting too much has the same effect as not highlighting at all: Nothing in the text stands out any more than anything else.*

3. Explain that the key to effective highlighting is to engage with the text actively. Say: *Imagine the text is really a source you're interviewing. You are a journalist, and your job is to track the fi e W's and one H of this news story! Do you know about the fi e W's and one H? Th y are: who, what, where, when, why, how.*

4. Use a well-known event or story to demonstrate the 5 W's and 1 H. This might be an event you've recently covered in history, a story you've recently covered in literature, or a story you know is familiar to your students, such as a folk tale, fairy tale, or fable.

5. Have students define who, what, where, when, why, and how for that event or story.

6. Next, discuss what students should look for as answers to these six questions. Distribute Handout 1.2: What Should I Highlight?: A Guide to Active Reading and Annotating. You might make a list on the board, but you might also have them follow along on the handout.

7. Review the "Pro Tips" on Handout 1.2 with your students. Tell students that these skills will be valuable as they continue their design thinking journey.

How Would That Feel?: A Guide to Building Empathy

Suggested Materials

- Student computer and Internet access to articles about climate change, such as:
  - "Climate Change and Housing: Will a Rising Tide Sink All Homes?" by Krishna Rao (available at https://www.zillow.com/research/climate-change-underwater-homes-12890)
  - "Implications of Global Climate Change for Housing, Human Settlements and Public Health" by S. Hales, M. Baker, P. Howden-Chapman, B. Menne, R. Woodruff, and A. Woodward (available at https://www.ncbi.nlm.nih.gov/pubmed/18351228)
  - "Adapting to Climate Change: Cities and the Urban Poor" (available at https://www.huduser.gov/portal/pdredge/pdr_edge_hudpartrpt_120111_1.html)

- Student Design Notebooks
- Student copies of Handout 1.3: Building Empathy and Connecting With People in Different Circumstances

Sequence

1. Introduce empathy to students: *Empathy is the ability to understand and share the feelings of another.*
2. Ask students to create a class brainstorm of what all humans care about. You might prompt them or add on to the conversation with the following:
   - food;
   - shelter;
   - safety from danger: natural disasters, wild animals, crime;
   - taking care of children;
   - being with our families;
   - seeing friends;
   - enjoyment/entertainment;
   - working toward personal goals;
   - happiness;
   - freedom from fear;
   - freedom from pain;
   - health;

- o   prosperity/financial security;
- o   learning and education;
- o   making the world a better place;
- o   helping others;
- o   art;
- o   community;
- o   connection; and/or
- o   right and wrong/ethics.

3.   Provide students with access to articles about climate change (see Suggested Materials list). The class can all read the same article, or you can assign different articles to different students or groups of students.

4.   Distribute Handout 1.3: Building Empathy and Connecting With People in Different Circumstances for students to complete in reference to the articles they read.

Writing a Response to a Problem and Creating a Problem Statement

Suggested Materials

- Students' notes and/or annotated copies of articles from Mini-Lesson 1.3
- Student Design Notebooks
- Student copies of Handout 1.4: Short Paragraph Writing Template, Handout 1.5: Long Paragraph Writing Template, or 1.6: Multi-Paragraph Writing Template (depending on the length of response students will be writing)
- Student copies of Handout 1.7: Transition Words and Phrases
- Student copies of Handout 1.8: Tools for Defining the Problem

Sequence

1. Tell students that they have already completed the first stage of Step 1 of design thinking by empathizing with people. They will now complete the second stage: setting up the problem.
2. Distribute the appropriate handout (1.4, 1.5, or 1.6), depending on the length of responses you would like students to write. Instruct them to follow the steps of the handout(s) to first take notes and then write out full-sentence responses from their ordered notes.
3. (Optional) Once students have written drafts, distribute Handout 1.7, and ask them to add appropriate transition words and phrases to their writing. Students might do this for their own papers, or they might switch papers with a classmate to provide suggestions for using transitions. This step can be skipped for classes running short on time.
4. Instruct students to proofread their drafts once they have finished writing them.
5. Next, distribute Handout 1.8: Tools for Defining the Problem. Tell students that in order to be successful in solving a problem using design thinking, they need to frame the problem in a certain way. Point out the checklist at the top of the handout.
6. Read the sample problem statements with your class, and ask students to apply the checklist to each statement. Help students see that it would be very challenging to implement and assess the success of the problem statements with too few and too many limitations.

7. Direct students to the section of the handout called "Writing Frames for Your Problem Statement." Invite them to experiment with each frame by filling in the elements in brackets from the written responses they just completed. As they work, circulate and offer suggestions and support.

8. Once students have problem statements, instruct them to apply the checklist. Depending on the time available, this can be done in small groups (less time) or one by one as each student reads his or her problem statement aloud (more time).

9. Once each student has a successful problem statement, congratulate the class on this very important step and let students know that now they have the foundation they need to put their empathy into action.

WHAT SHOULD I SAY?: A GUIDE TO EFFECTIVE FEEDBACK

Suggested Materials

- Students' written responses created in Mini-Lesson 1.4
- Student copies of Handout 1.9: What Should I Say?: A Guide to Effective Feedback

Sequence

1. Tell students that design thinking is most effective when thinkers collaborate and combine their ideas. To achieve the benefits of collaboration, they will be offering one another feedback on writing at various points in this unit. Tell them that in this mini-lesson they will learn best practices for giving helpful feedback and building a collaborative atmosphere in the classroom.

2. Tell students they will be learning the four traits of effective feedback and how to provide it. Effective feedback:
   o is necessary and timely,
   o is specific and actionable,
   o distinguishes between facts and our reactions, and
   o is presented the way we ourselves would want to hear it.

3. Provide more detail about the first trait: Point out that necessary and timely feedback helps us move forward from where we are. Feedback that we can't apply at our current stage of writing isn't necessary or timely. Specific and actionable feedback helps us see the solution in the problem. Walk students through the following example: *If my peer has just shared a fi st draft with me, the following feedback would be necessary, specific, and actionable: "I only heard one supporting detail in the second paragraph, although the other paragraphs have three supporting details." It would also be timely because my peer is about to work on revising the fi st draft, and that will be the perfect opportunity to add the needed details. On the other hand, pointing out a misspelling in my peer's outline isn't necessary or timely because this will steal her focus away from ideas, which are the most important at the outlining stage.*

4. Show students how helpful feedback also distinguishes between facts and our reactions by providing them with examples (see Figure 1).

Helpful Reaction	Reaction Stated as Fact
This sentence **didn't grab my attention**.	This sentence **is** boring.
I was confused in the conclusion; I wasn't sure if you agreed or disagreed with the author of the article.	Your conclusion **is** confusing.

Figure 1. Helpful feedback versus reactions stated as fact.

5. Ask students: *Distinguishing between statements of fact and reactions helps us deliver feedback in the way we ourselves would want to hear it. Would we like hearing the second type of statement about something into which we had put hard work?*

6. Tell students that distinguishing between statements of fact and reactions also helps provide actionable feedback. Invite them to notice that the helpful reactions hold a clue as to how the work can be improved. We give feedback in order to be helpful. A judgment about writing is usually a conversation ender; however, our reaction can often be a conversation starter.

7. Distribute Handout 1.9: What Should I Say?: A Guide to Effective Feedback. Have students form groups of 2–4 so that they can trade papers (the responses they wrote in Mini-Lesson 1.4) and offer constructive feedback utilizing the handout.

CONCLUDING ACTIVITIES

Journal Prompts for Student Reflection

- What did you learn by reading the article?
- Were you surprised by anything you read in the article?
- What do you like about the problem statement(s) you wrote?
- What skills and talents did you find yourself using in this module?
- What part of this module did you really enjoy?
- What part of this module did you find really challenging?

Suggested Assignments

- Thoughtfully respond to any three of the journal prompts; include these in your Design Notebook.
- Write a final draft of the response to the article to be included in your Design Notebook.
- Create a work of art—a drawing, painting, collage, or graphic design—to accompany the problem statement. This might be an illustration of the solution, or a logo or motto for the problem statement.

Suggested Blog Posts

- Giving Peer Feedback: What NOT To Do
- The Top 10 Reasons We Need Affordable Housing Now
- The Surprising Effects of Climate Change No One Is Talking About
- 7 Innovative Ideas for Solving the Global Housing Crisis
- How to Write an Effective Problem Statement in 5 Steps
- The Real Cost of Climate Change

Handout 1.1

Welcome Letter

Dear QUIRC Scholar:

We are thrilled to inform you that you have been chosen to join our underwater engineering and design team. Welcome aboard! We're delighted to have you as part of our Research and Development Team at the Quinn University Innovation and Research Center.

This year we had triple our usual number of applicants, making our selection process quite difficult. Thank you for your patience during our deliberation. Your application stood head and shoulders above the rest; we know your contribution to our efforts will be invaluable.

About You

First, I wanted to outline the attributes you have that I think will bring the most value to a project like this. Then I'll share some of the specific ways those could translate into our team's success.

Based on your application and recommendations, it was apparent that:

- You are very creative. You have a unique ability to observe a problem and develop multiple strategies to solve that problem.
- You are resilient. When an idea doesn't work out the way you planned, you know how to learn from your mistakes without letting setbacks hold you back.
- You are committed to following through; you don't give up. We were particularly impressed by your commitment to seeing a project through to the end, even when it was difficult or seemed impossible to many.

At QUIRC, we solve real-world problems with creativity and ingenuity. That's why we think you'll fit right in!

About This Project

Our latest project is far from dry. I'll put it in the terms of a simple equation:

a growing population + a finite planet + rising sea levels = where do people live?

In response to this problem, lots of cities build up—sometimes as high as 100 floors and tens of millions of dollars! That's great if you're a gajillionaire with a private express elevator.

What about the rest of us? At QUIRC, we believe all of the world's people have the right to safe, affordable, sustainable housing. So we asked a simple question: *What if we built down? Specifically, under water!*

Your role as a QUIRC Scholar will be to design and engineer the living, learning, and working spaces of the very first permanent undersea habitats.

COULD YOU LIVE UNDERWATER? © Taylor & Francis Group

Handout 1.1, Continued.

We know this brings a lot of challenges with it. How will people breathe, eat, generate electricity, or even just survive the pressure? But we're confident that our crack team of big thinkers in science, technology, engineering, math, and design—which now includes you!—will meet the challenges and provide a solution.

Your Assignment

Using your problem-solving skills and innovative thinking, your job will be to design, build, and test a prototype of a permanent undersea habitat.

Once you build and test your prototype, you'll have a chance to share your design and your findings with the rest of the QUIRC community and the larger world, using video and social media.

Ready to, uh, "dive" in?

1. First, you will conduct research. Through a series of open-ended questions, we want you to put your keen insights and critical thinking skills to use as a foundation throughout the rest of this project.

2. Next, we have curated a series of tests and experiments designed to help you explore the various properties of water so you can create your design prototype from a place of deep understanding regarding the challenges we are facing.

3. Then, using the wisdom gained through your research, experimentation, and ideating phase, you will build a prototype underwater city using simple engineering materials like cardboard, tinfoil, duct tape, straws, etc.

4. Finally, it's time to test your design! As we are only in the very beginning phase of understanding the challenges of living underwater, the data you acquire through your test will give the entire engineering and design team valuable understanding regarding the next steps we should take to solve our design and engineering problem.

Sharing and Recording Your Work

We'll be looking for your test results, your reflections, and your revisions throughout social media with the hashtag #couldyouliveunderwater. As we said, you have the unique attributes of a successful underwater engineer. We wait in anticipation of your results.

As you work you'll also be creating a Design Notebook as a handy place to:

- organize your research,
- outline your plan,
- record your findings, and
- track your progress on your prototype.

Handout 1.1, Continued.

Don't be afraid to mind-map in the margins, brainstorm in the blank spaces, and doodle designs wherever they'll fit! This notebook is a place to capture all of your ideas, even the crazy ones.

I can't wait to see what you contribute to this project!

Best of luck!

Sincerely,

Mariana T. Sandoval

Mariana T. Sandoval
President, Quinn University

P.S. Be safe in your experiments and conscious of how you use water—it's one of our most precious resources! And if you do any experimenting in the ocean directly, I advise you not to trust any giant squid. Alas, I speak from experience, which is why I'm no longer a QUIRC field researcher myself and am instead stuck behind this desk . . . but that's another story.

Handout 1.2

What Should I Highlight?: A Guide to Active Reading and Annotating

Directions: The key to effective highlighting is to imagine that the text you are using to research is really a source you're interviewing. The handout includes some tips of what to look for as you analyze the 5 W's (who, what, where, when, why) and 1 H (how) of the sources you use for this project.

The 5 W's and 1 H		
Who	animals species people groups organizations	schools governments teams nations cultures
What	discovery invention demonstration event protest fight battle war disaster	agreement partnership treaty law solution pattern change beginning ending
Where	ecosystems biomes geographic landmarks cities regions	states nations continents planets
When	date month season year geological era (the Jurassic Period)	historical era (the Middle Ages) thought era (the Enlightenment) social and political era (the Civil Rights Movement) ongoing event (the Great Depression)
Why	question goal objective misunderstanding difference of opinion injustice	fear power struggle love new idea curiosity
How	discussion cooperation communication legislation	intimidation coercion violence

Handout 1.2, Continued.

Pro Tips

- Read the whole paragraph before highlighting so you can choose the elements that contain the most information!
- Highlight words and phrases instead of complete sentences. The more spaces there are between two highlighted sections, the more those sections will draw your eye.
- Annotate (take notes) in the margins. Ask questions, summarize an idea, or write down what the situation reminds you of.
- Use symbols in your annotations. Try: ! for surprising information, ? for confusing passages, :-) for a positive outcome or something you agree with, :-(for a negative outcome or something you disagree with, or * for something that seems really important. You can create your own system of annotations to make active reading a faster, more streamlined process.

Handout 1.3
Building Empathy and Connecting With People in Different Circumstances

Directions: Empathy is the ability to understand and share the feelings of another. Use this worksheet along with an article or story you have accessed during your research. Answer the questions about the person or people featured in the article or story.

1. Who is most affected by the issue at hand?

2. How are you different from the people you read about? Think about location, family, and lifestyle.

3. What do you have in common with the people you read about? Consider needs, wants, fears, hopes and dreams, family, and friends.

4. What happened to the people you read about?

5. What clues were there about how these people felt? What did they say and do?

Handout 1.3, Continued.

6. What is your best guess about what else these people probably felt? What is your reasoning for this guess?

7. If this had happened to you, you would feel . . .

8. If this had happened to you, you would want . . .

9. What do you think is most important to these people? If they could make one request of someone in power, what would it be?

Handout 1.4

Short Paragraph Writing Template

Directions: A writing template is like a picture frame for your thoughts. It gives you a way to organize your ideas and make writing easier. This template will help you plan and write a short paragraph response to an article you've read. Use a separate sheet of paper if necessary.

Step 1

Jot down notes to answer the following questions. You don't have to write complete sentences.

1.   Who were the people you read about?

2.   Where do these people live?

3.   What kind of problem have they been facing?

4.   How did this problem start?

5.   Why does this problem exist? What causes it?

6.   What is your idea for a solution to this problem?

Handout 1.4, Continued.

Step 2

Use the template below to organize your thoughts and put them into complete sentences. Wherever you see a number, replace it with the ideas you wrote down for that number in Step 1.

We learned that [1] who live [2] have been facing the problem of [3] ever since [4]. This problem is caused by [5]. We want to solve the problem by [6].

Step 3

Add transition words and phrases to your paragraph to make your ideas clear. Use Handout 1.7: Transition Words and Phrases.

Handout 1.5
Long Paragraph Writing Template

Directions: A writing template is like a picture frame for your thoughts. It gives you a way to organize your ideas and make writing easier. This template will help you plan and write a long paragraph response to an article you've read. Use a separate sheet of paper if necessary.

Step 1

Jot down notes to respond to the following prompts. You don't have to write complete sentences.

1. Summarize the problem in the article(s).

2. Explain how long the problem has been going on.

3. Describe the worst part of the problem.

4. Explain the cause of the problem.

5. Summarize your idea for a solution to the problem.

Handout 1.5, Continued.

Step 2

Write out the ideas from Step 1 in complete sentences. Follow the order from 1–5.

Step 3

Add transition words and phrases to your paragraph to make your ideas clear. Use Handout 1.7: Transition Words and Phrases.

Handout 1.6
Multi-Paragraph Writing Template

Directions: A writing template is like a picture frame for your thoughts. It gives you a way to organize your ideas and make writing easier. This template will help you plan and write a multi-paragraph response to an article you've read. Use a separate sheet of paper if necessary.

Step 1

Jot down notes to respond to the following prompts and questions. You don't have to write complete sentences.

1. Summarize the problem in the article.

    a. Details about the people and where they live:

    b. Details of what is happening to them:

    c. Details of how their lives are affected:

2. Explain the causes of the problem.

    a. Historical causes of this problem or the pattern it's part of:

    b. Recent changes that have caused this problem:

    c. How has this problem gotten worse lately?

3. What solutions have been tried or suggested for this problem?

Handout 1.6, Continued.

a. Who, if anyone, has been trying to solve this problem?

b. How have people been trying to solve this problem?

c. Have the solutions worked? Do they seem like they will work in the future?

4. What is your idea for a solution to the problem(s)?

a. Restate the problem and its causes.

b. Describe your solution.

c. Explain why your solution will help.

Step 2

Write out the ideas from Step 1 in complete sentences on a separate sheet of paper. Follow the order from 1 through 4, using all of the A, B, and C ideas in order before moving onto the next number. Whenever you get to a new number, start a new paragraph.

Step 3

Add transition words and phrases to your paragraphs to make your ideas clear. Use Handout 1.7: Transition Words and Phrases.

Handout 1.7
Transition Words and Phrases

Directions: Transition words and phrases are like traffic signs: They tell the reader when to keep moving, when to slow down, and when to change direction. Choose the words and phrases that will help you connect and clarify your ideas for your readers.

Tell your reader about causes and effects:

one reason	the most surprising effect	which resulted in
another reason	as a result	predictably
one cause	leading to	immediately
another cause	causing	setting off
one effect	resulting in	precipitating
another effect	which led to	effectively making
the most important reason/		
cause/effect		

Tell your reader about a related idea:

in addition	moreover	also
additionally	similarly	furthermore

Show your reader a contrast or difference:

on the other hand	contrary to expectation	yet
in contrast	although (A is B, X is Y)	however
surprisingly	but	even though

Show your reader the sequence of events:

suddenly	next	eventually
immediately	when	finally
imminently	while	after
soon	shortly thereafter	during
then	years later	

Show your reader a negative consequence:

unfortunately	upsettingly
disastrously	regrettably
tragically	

Show your reader a positive consequence or possibility:

fortunately	thanks to (person, group, or action)
wonderfully	with support from (person, group, or action)
hopefully	

Handout 1.8
Tools for Defining the Problem

Directions: Use the tips on this handout to assist you with developing your problem statement.

Checklist for Your Problem Statement

- ✓ Make it a question.
- ✓ Make it about an action (teach, create, provide, build, etc.).
- ✓ Focus on people.
- ✓ Make it about specific people, places, and goals.

Sample Problem Statements

- **Too few limitations:** How can we keep all pigs safe all the time?
- **Too many limitations:** How can we provide the three little pigs with shelters that are octagonal, 64 cubic feet, and purple?
- **Just the right size:** How can we provide the three pigs with shelters that will keep them safe from the wolf?

Writing Frames for Your Problem Statement

1. How can we provide [people] with [goal]?
2. How can we create [resource] that helps [people] do [goal]?
3. How can we build [resource] that ensures [people] can [goal]?
4. How can we teach [people] to [goal] with [resource]?

Handout 1.9

What Should I Say?: A Guide to Effective Feedback

Directions: Use the checklists on this handout to assist you when providing peer feedback.

Feedback Checklist

- ✓ Is it necessary and timely?
- ✓ Is it specific and actionable?
- ✓ Does it distinguish between a fact and my reaction?
- ✓ Is it presented the way I would want to hear it?

Structure

- ✓ Is there a topic sentence? Can I tell what the writing will cover from the first paragraph?
- ✓ Does the author wrap up his or her thoughts in some way at the end of the writing?
- ✓ Are there transition words and phrases that help the reader track ideas and move smoothly from one idea to the next?
- ✓ Could elements be reordered to make the writing more clear?
- ✓ Is there any helpful advice I can give to improve the structure?

Content

- ✓ Are the ideas clear? Can I list the main topics or categories that I heard about?
- ✓ Are there specific details, such as people, places, events, causes, effects, or examples?
- ✓ Do the ideas make sense? Are they well-reasoned and logically explained?
- ✓ Do the ideas go together, or are they unrelated/contradictory?
- ✓ Am I confused about anything?
- ✓ Is there any helpful advice I can give to improve the content?

Language

- ✓ Does the author avoid repetition of words and phrases where possible?
- ✓ Does the author use specific action words and phrases that help me understand the situation?
- ✓ Is there any helpful advice I can give to improve the language?

Presentation

- ✓ Is the handwriting easy to read?
- ✓ Is there a title?
- ✓ Are all the intended words present? Have extra words been removed?
- ✓ Is there any helpful advice I can give to improve the presentation?

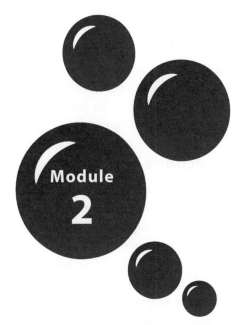

RESEARCH AND IDEATION

Objectives

In this module, students will conduct research about underwater living. They will direct their research based on guiding questions, and they will also understand how to organize important findings. Students will learn effective methods for selecting reliable sources, taking notes, and paraphrasing what they read.

Overview

Students begin with a class/individual brain dump about the challenges of living underwater. Following this, they are given a list of open-ended questions and can choose which ones they will research.

Using their chosen questions, students research and take notes. If students will be selecting their own research materials, the teacher presents Mini-Lesson 2.2: Where Can I Find Accurate Information?: A Guide to Choosing Reliable Resources. If any online research will be conducted, the teacher should present Mini-Lesson 2.3: How Do I Get Answers on the Web?: A Guide to Effective Online Research. Research can be conducted in class using the web, classroom books, or books the teacher brings in or asks parents to obtain from the local library. Alternatively or in addition, classes could go together to the school library, a nearby library, or even a science/learning center as a field trip.

At the conclusion of their research, students present their findings to the class either informally through discussion, or more formally through creative projects.

 DOI: 10.4324/9781003233831-5

Tech Connections

Students can write and post on the classroom blog and then share their posts on social media, using the hashtag #couldyouliveunderwater. Photos and videos of the final presentations can also be posted on the classroom blog and/or on social media using that same hashtag.

Writing Connections

If time permits, students can write research reports, using Handout 2.6: Outlining a Research Report. We recommend that students work in groups of 4–5 to cowrite research reports as part of the Concluding Activities for this module. Each student can author one paragraph of the report, and by collaborating on the process with their peers, they will get an introduction to the research report writing process in a fun, low-pressure atmosphere. There are also suggested blog posts in the Concluding Activities section for those classrooms keeping a blog. Encourage students to use the provided blog post titles as inspiration for what they will write.

Time Frame

Time Period	One Class Period (45–90 min.)	One Extended Period (90–120 min.)	One Week (5 Class Periods)
Activities	• Mini-Lesson 2.1: Open-Ended Questions for Research • Mini-Lesson 2.4: What's the Most Important Idea?: A Guide to Paraphrasing and Taking Notes • Students read and research • Discuss and share findings with the class	• Mini-Lesson 2.1: Open-Ended Questions for Research • Mini-Lesson 2.2: Where Can I Find Accurate Information?: A Guide to Choosing Reliable Resources • Mini-Lesson 2.4: What's the Most Important Idea?: A Guide to Paraphrasing and Taking Notes • Students read and research • Discuss and share findings with the class	• Mini-Lesson 2.1: Open-Ended Questions for Research • Mini-Lesson 2.2: Where Can I Find Accurate Information?: A Guide to Choosing Reliable Resources • Mini-Lesson 2.3: How Do I Get Answers on the Web?: A Guide to Effective Online Research • Mini-Lesson 2.4: What's the Most Important Idea?: A Guide to Paraphrasing and Taking Notes • Students read and research • Students write research reports using Handout 2.6: Outlining a Research Report

Time Period, *continued.*	One Class Period (45–90 min.), *continued.*	One Extended Period (90–120 min.), *continued.*	One Week (5 Class Periods), *continued*
Activities, *continued.*			• Discuss and share findings with the class • Concluding Activities

One Class Period: The teacher presents Mini-Lesson 2.1: Open-Ended Questions for Research, as well as Mini-Lesson 2.4: What's the Most Important Idea?: A Guide to Paraphrasing and Taking Notes. Students work in small groups to read materials provided and take notes about as many questions as they can. Findings are shared through a class discussion at the end of the period and students sharing their notes orally. Alternatively, students work in groups to research on the web or in classroom/library books to answer the questions they're most interested in. Findings are shared through a class discussion at the end of the period and students sharing their notes orally.

One Extended Period: The teacher presents Mini-Lesson 2.1: Open-Ended Questions for Research, and the class uses brainstorms and mind maps to generate questions about the ocean. The teacher presents the Mini-Lesson 2.2: Where Can I Find Accurate Information?: A Guide to Choosing Reliable Resources, along with Mini Lesson 2.4: What's the Most Important Idea?: A Guide to Paraphrasing and Taking Notes. Students work in small groups to read materials provided and take notes about as many questions as they can. Each group creates a short presentation about its findings to share orally with the rest of the class. Alternatively, students work in groups to research on the web or in classroom books to answer the questions they're most interested in. Each group creates a short presentation about its findings to share orally with the rest of the class.

One Week: The teacher presents Mini-Lesson 2.1: Open-Ended Questions for Research, and the class uses brainstorms and mind maps to generate questions about the ocean. The teacher presents the Mini-Lesson 2.2: Where Can I Find Accurate Information?: A Guide to Choosing Reliable Resources, along with Mini-Lesson 2.3: How Do I Get Answers on the Web?: A Guide to Effective Online Research, and Mini Lesson 2.4: What's the Most Important Idea?: A Guide to Paraphrasing and Taking Notes. Students work in groups or individually to conduct research in class and/or at home. They take notes, organize their notes, and then create presentations of their findings to share on Day 5.

- **Day 1:** Introduce open-ended questions and invite students to add their own. Complete Mini-Lessons 2.1–2.4.
- **Day 2:** Research and take notes.
- **Day 3:** Research and take notes.
- **Day 4:** Organize research and create presentations and/or reports.
- **Day 5:** Share and discuss presentations. Concluding Activities.

Open-Ended Questions for Research

Suggested Materials

- Student Design Notebooks
- Student copies of Handout 2.1: What Do Designers Need to Know About the Ocean?

Sequence

1. Ask students: What do humans need to survive on land? Think about all of the aspects of life to account for. What would humans need to live underwater? Consider . . .
   - food,
   - waste,
   - security,
   - entertainment,
   - learning,
   - health,
   - water pressure,
   - temperature, and
   - communication below and above water.

2. Ask students to further consider the following questions. (These will be explored in greater depth during Module 4, so the intention for the questions in this module should be simply to have a lively discussion that helps students think in broad strokes about these topics.)
   - How can these needs be met underwater?
   - Are there any advantages or disadvantages to living underwater rather than on land?
   - What are the design challenges of building underwater?
   - In what ways can water be considered a design element?
   - What dangers does the ocean hold for engineered structures?
   - What dangers does the ocean hold for human survival?

3. Distribute Handout 2.1: What Do Designers Need to Know About the Ocean? to provide students with foundational knowledge about conditions underwater, as well as ideas for further topics to research. This can be an opportunity for practicing read-aloud and listening skills. Classes may want to popcorn read: Students read a sentence or two aloud when the teacher randomly calls on them. Alternatively, students might volunteer to read a paragraph each.

Mini-Lesson 2.2

WHERE CAN I FIND ACCURATE INFORMATION?: A GUIDE TO CHOOSING RELIABLE RESOURCES

Suggested Materials

- Student computer and Internet access
- Student copies of Handout 2.2: Where Can I Find Accurate Information?

Sequence

1. Distribute Handout 2.2: Where Can I Find Accurate Information? Briefly introduce the three types of sources: primary, secondary, and tertiary. Encourage students to utilize primary sources where available, and discuss what forms these might take: interviews, journals, letters, etc.

2. Then, take students through the three key criteria of finding reliable resources. Reliable sources should be written and published by people and organizations that are knowledgeable, unbiased, and held to a high standard of scholarship.

3. If time permits, find examples of two or three sources, so that students can practice going through the checklist. This can be done as a class or in small groups. Suggested materials include:
   o a dictionary,
   o a blog post chosen at random from the web,
   o an online encyclopedia,
   o an opinion piece in a newspaper,
   o a textbook or activity book from the classroom, and
   o a social media post.

4. Walk the students through red flags—the details that should make them question the reliability of a source:
   o **Red Flag 1:** No credentials are supplied for the author/publisher.
   o **Red Flag 2:** The information has been published for commercial purposes, for example, a website selling SCUBA diving adventure packages.
   o **Red Flag 3:** The author uses argumentative language, for example, "Obviously, anyone who disagrees with this idea is a giant squid!"
   o **Red Flag 4:** A website or blog published by a private individual with no affiliation with a larger organization that you have reason to trust.

How Do I Get Answers on the Web?: A Guide to Effective Online Research

Suggested Materials

- Student computer and Internet access
- Overhead projector (optional)
- Student copies of Handout 2.3: How Do I Get Answers on the Web?

Sequence

1. Discuss the steps outlined on Handout 2.3: How Do I Get Answers on the Web? You can deliver this material via lecture and discussion, in which case students should follow along with the handout. Alternatively, you can walk them through the process using a computer and overhead projector.
2. Instruct students to use the steps on Handout 2.3 to begin researching each of the open-ended research questions from Mini-Lesson 2.1.
3. If time and resources permit, instruct students to conduct their own queries while you observe and offer support.

Mini-Lesson 2.4

WHAT'S THE MOST IMPORTANT IDEA?: A GUIDE TO PARAPHRASING AND TAKING NOTES

Suggested Materials

- A fairy tale, fable, folk tale, or other story that your class knows well for reference (a printed copy is *not* necessary)
- Student computer and Internet access
- Nonfiction books about the ocean from your school/local library
- Student Design Notebooks
- Student copies of Handout 2.4: A Guide to Paraphrasing and Taking Notes
- Student copies of Handout 2.5: Suggested Articles for Research About Climate Change

Sequence

1. Explain to students the purpose of research: *When you research, your job is to take a lot of information from different sources and put it together for a single goal. Th s goal might be to inform, persuade, or entertain. Whatever your goal, though, your job is to explain what you've learned from your research. That means you not only need to find i formation, but you also need to:*
    o read it,
    o understand it,
    o organize it,
    o state your conclusions, and
    o explain your conclusions.

2. Tell students that they will be presenting their findings to the class at the end of their research, as well as using the information they find to complete the upcoming steps of the design thinking process.

3. Distribute Handout 2.4: A Guide to Paraphrasing and Taking Notes, and guide students through it, or have them work in groups or pairs to read the handout as you circulate to pose questions and offer support.

4. Invite the class to help you take notes on a story you all know. As students suggest key ideas, model how to write down these ideas briefly, possibly using symbols to speed up the process. Imagine using "The Three Little Pigs" as an example; your notes might look like this:

3 pigs leave home to make their lives in the world
2 = want to play → don't care about houses
1 = serious; wants strong house
First → builds house of straw
Second → builds house of sticks
Third → builds house of bricks

5. Discuss any questions students have about taking notes and using note-cards.
6. Invite students to begin their research on the Internet or by utilizing books you have collected, or arrange for them to visit the library. If students are conducting research online, distribute Handout 2.5: Suggested Articles for Research About Climate Change.

CONCLUDING ACTIVITIES

Suggested Projects for Presentation

- Create a written presentation to share research findings. (*Note*. Students might work together in groups and each create a different paragraph of a research report, using Handout 2.6: Outlining a Research Report.)
- Create a work of art—a drawing, painting, collage, or graphic design—to share research findings. This might be an infographic of key information, a graph of data, or an illustration of a principle, process, or concept learned about during research.

Journal Prompts for Student Reflection

- What did you enjoy about researching?
- What did you find challenging about conducting your research?
- How did you get your best information? A certain book? A certain webpage?
- Where did you take your notes? Did this work for you?
- The next time you conduct research, what would you like to do differently?
- Would anything have made the research process easier or more effective for you?
- What advice would you give to someone else who is about to start a research project?

Suggested Assignments

- Thoughtfully respond to any three of the journal prompts; include these in your Design Notebook.
- Continue research.
- Work on outlining the research presentation.
- Work on drafting the research presentation.

Suggested Blog Posts

- 5 Common Research Mistakes and How to Avoid Them
- How to Get the Most Out of Online Research
- The 7 Most Surprising Facts About the Ocean
- What's It Really Like on the Ocean Floor?
- Could You Live Underwater? The 3 Biggest Ocean Design Challenges
- The Top 10 Reasons You're Glad You Live on Dry Land

Handout 2.1
What Do Designers Need to Know About the Ocean?

270 million years ago, the land formations on Earth were connected in one super-continent that scientists have named *Pangea*. The ocean circulated around this huge land-mass until the landmass broke apart, separating the ocean into five separate parts; the Southern, Arctic, Atlantic, Pacific, and Indian Oceans.

These five bodies of water combined cover 70% of the Earth's surface. Despite the ocean being the defining feature of Earth, it remains mostly unexplored by humans.

To better understand the ocean—and the challenges of building structures below its surface—it can be helpful to draw some similarities between conditions underwater and conditions on land.

Terrain

Just like land, the ocean's floor is covered with features like valleys, mountain ranges, trenches, plains, and rifts. Thus, one challenge designers will face is choosing an appropriate terrain as a building site.

Water: The Air of the Sea

The water that makes up the ocean can be compared to the air that surrounds us on land. Both are technically considered fluid because they both flow, move along in the form of currents, and take the shape of whatever container they are in.

Accordingly, underwater designers and builders must consider the properties of water at various depths, in the same way skyscraper designers and builders must consider the properties of air at various heights.

There are two key difference between the air we breathe and the water in the ocean. The first is that ocean water is made of up H_2O (two hydrogen atoms and an oxygen atom cova-lently bound together to form a water molecule), while the air we breathe is primarily nitro-gen and oxygen gas. Another key difference between our air and ocean water is that ocean water is full of salt. We call this phenomenon, the concentration of salt in water, *salinity*.

Want Salt With That?

The salinity of the ocean is why ocean water has such unusual chemical and physical properties. Have you ever wondered why the ocean doesn't freeze? Water's freezing point decreases as its salinity increases. The density of ocean water is also affected by its salinity. However, salinity is not constant throughout the entire ocean. Different regions of ocean have different salt concentrations. This means that the temperature and density of these regions also vary.

Handout 2.1, Continued.

Going With the Flow

The interactions among these different regions creates the deep currents in the ocean. These deep ocean currents can be compared to air currents on land. Imagine a skyscraper pummeled by the strong winds produced by air currents. Can you see why an understanding of ocean currents is necessary to underwater designers?

Above deep currents there are surface currents. Just as on land the wind circulates air and promotes seed and pollen dispersion, the wind also circulates the surface of the ocean. Surface currents affect the distribution of nutrients and the balance of the ocean's ecosystem.

Both deep currents and surface currents affect the circulation of the ocean. So does the Earth's gravitational relationship with the moon, which we experience as tides that vary according to the phase of the moon.

Another commonality between the ocean and land is a dependence on photosynthesis for oxygen creation and food propagation. Plants are a vital part of the food chain on land and in the ocean, supporting all life from its simplest forms to its most complex.

Changing Salinity, Changing Oceans

The salinity of the ocean is affected by many things, such as melting glaciers, erosion, and inflow from rivers and streams causing fresh water (water with no or very low salt concentration) to interact with ocean water.

The factors that affect salinity, and in turn, temperature, density, and currents, are not constant. As our global climate warms, the properties and behavior of the ocean will change. These changes promise to affect the way humans live. Everything from where we can safely build homes to what we eat will be impacted. Oceans have always been central to our overall diet. From harvesting seaweed to catching fish and using sea salt as a flavor enhancer, our culinary lives rely on the ocean.

Now that you understand the ocean's unique properties and similarities to land, you can apply this knowledge to the rest of your research as you design your solution to the problem of living underwater.

Handout 2.2

Where Can I Find Accurate Information?: A Guide to Choosing Reliable Resources

Directions: Reliable sources should be written and published by people and organizations that are knowledgeable, unbiased, and held to a high standard of scholarship.

Knowledgeable

- Who is the author and publisher of this information?
- What are the credentials of the author/publisher?
- Does my common sense tell me that this author/publisher is likely to be knowledgeable about this topic?

Red Flag: No credentials are supplied for the author/publisher.

Unbiased

- Does this article contain data, quotes from experts, or excerpts from primary sources with citations?
- Does my common sense tell me that the author is offering facts as opposed to opinions?

Red Flag: The information has been published for commercial purposes, for example, a website selling SCUBA diving adventure packages.

Red Flag: The author uses argumentative language, for example, "Obviously, anyone who disagrees with this idea is a giant squid!"

Held to a High Standard of Scholarship

- Does the publisher have a responsibility to the public, like a government organization?
- Does the publisher have a reputation to uphold, like an educational publisher, a university, a research center, or a well-known encyclopedia?

Red Flag: A website or blog is published by a private individual with no affiliation with a larger organization that you have reason to trust.

Pro Tip: Check out nonfiction books from the library about your topic. When researching on the web, visit the websites of well-known encyclopedias, government agencies, and universities.

Handout 2.3

How Do I Get Answers on the Web?: A Guide
to Effective Online Research

- **Step 1:** Start by typing one of your open-ended research questions into a search engine.
- **Step 2:** Explore the first page of articles returned. Right-click on their titles and open them in new tabs so that you can keep your original search page accessible.
- **Step 3:** Briefly scan each web page to determine whether it's worth reading. Do this using your accurate information checklist (Handout 2.2)!
- **Step 4:** Once you've determined the sites from the first page of results that are worth reading, copy and paste their URLs into a word processing document under the heading of your query.

Troubleshooting

- If you find fewer than two useable sources for any query, you can move on to the second page of results or click on any of the suggested queries down at the bottom of the search page.
- You might also try removing extraneous words, leaving only the keywords, such as "humans living under pressure ocean."

Complete these steps for each of the remaining questions you intend to research.

Shortcuts

- If you find a source that is particularly helpful, you can always conduct a search within that resource if it offers a search bar.
- Similarly, you can use your search engine to search within that source by including the name of the source in your query.

Avoid Detours

The Internet is a vast and wonderful place. It can be easy to get lost by following a trail of hyperlinks. The most important guideline is to *click with intention*. Don't click on a link simply because it's there; instead, click on the links that sound as though they will . . .
- ✓ provide needed background details,
- ✓ take you deeper into the topic you want to research, and
- ✓ be more relevant than the initial article you clicked on.

When following links . . .
- ✓ open new links in new tabs and keep the originals open, and
- ✓ record the URL before taking notes or gathering information from a site.

Handout 2.4
A Guide to Paraphrasing and Taking Notes

Step 1: Organize

Keep your questions in mind as you read and match the answers you get to those questions. A great way to do this is by using note cards. On one side of the note card (the unlined side, if applicable), write your research query. On the reverse side, take notes that help answer that question. At the top of the note card, write down the name of the source you're reading so you can cite it in your final presentation. That means you should start a new note card when you switch to a new source!

Step 2: Track What You Read

Take notes while you read. Read a few sentences or a few paragraphs, then pause and write down what you learned.

You might get frustrated pausing periodically while you read in order to write down notes. But it's a lot more frustrating to have to reread an entire source later because you forgot what you read the first time around!

Bonus: Taking notes while you read will help you efficiently identify sources that aren't going to help your research. If you've been reading along for a few paragraphs and there isn't any information that seems important enough to note down, you've just discovered that this source isn't helpful. Instead of continuing with it, you can move on to a different source. See how this saves you time?

Step 3: Find What's Relevant

Use Handout 1.2: What Should I Highlight? to help you track the key information in what you read. Remember, you're looking for answers to Who? What? Where? When? Why? and How?

Pay special attention to details, including:
* measurements,
* results of experiments,
* patterns,
* changes,
* reasons, and
* quotes from experts.

Write down these details—including the quotes from experts—exactly as they appear in the original text. Put quotation marks around text copied exactly from your source. If taking notes from a book, write down the page number these details appeared on.

Handout 2.4, Continued.

Step 4: Put Ideas Into Your Own Words

Good notes don't have to be in complete sentences! They simply have to grab the main idea of what we read in a way that we will recognize and understand when we return to it—even after a lot of time has passed.

Besides helping us pick out the most important details, understand what we're reading, and remember it, taking notes will ensure that we avoid plagiarism.

As researchers, scientists, and writers, we benefit from the hard work and great ideas of those who have come before us. Using what we have learned from others and acknowledging them through citations is part of the research process. Adding our own ideas onto the ideas of others is how we make progress!

On the other hand, plagiarism is the act of taking someone else's work and passing it off as our own. Taking notes as we research is the #1 best way to ensure that we don't plagiarize, even accidentally.

Handout 2.5

Suggested Articles for Research About Climate Change

"Adapting to Climate Change: Cities and the Urban Poor"

> https://www.huduser.gov/portal/pdredge/pdr_edge_hudpartrpt_120111_1.html

"Climate Change and Human Health"

> https://health2016.globalchange.gov/climate-change-and-human-health

"Climate Change and Health: Air Quality"

> https://www.nrdc.org/climate-change-and-health-air-quality#/map

"On the Climate Change Frontline: The Disappearing Fishing Villages of Bangladesh"

> https://www.theguardian.com/global-development/2017/jan/20/climate-change-frontline-disappearing-fishing-villages-bangladesh

"Rising Waters Threaten China's Rising Cities"

> https://www.nytimes.com/interactive/2017/04/07/world/asia/climate-change-china.html

"The Nature Conservancy: Papua New Guinea"

> https://www.tnc.org.hk/our-work/by-country/papua-new-guinea

"The Nature Conservancy: Preparing for the Worst of Climate Change in Papua New Guinea"

> https://www.tnc.org.hk/our-work/by-country/papua-new-guinea/preparing-for-the-worst-of-climate-change-in-papua-new-guinea

"Threatened By Rising Seas, Alaska Village Decides To Relocate"

> http://www.npr.org/sections/thetwo-way/2016/08/18/490519540/threatened-by-rising-seas-an-alaskan-village-decides-to-relocate

Handout 2.6

Outlining a Research Report

Directions: Use this outline template to organize your ideas for a research paper. The number of body paragraphs can be changed to suit your findings. Use a minimum of two body paragraphs.

1. Introductory Paragraph
   a. Background information about the topic (designing underwater)
   b. Purpose of the research paper (What were you hoping to find out and why?)
   c. Thesis statement (What will you cover in your body paragraphs?)

2. Body Paragraph
   a. Topic sentence (What will you cover in this paragraph?)
   b. Background information about this topic
   c. Details from your research
   d. Explanation of what the details mean and why they're significant
   e. Concluding sentence that restates the topic sentence

3. Body Paragraph
   a. Topic sentence (What will you cover in this paragraph?)
   b. Background information about this topic
   c. Details from your research
   d. Explanation of what the details mean and why they're significant
   e. Concluding sentence that restates the topic sentence

4. Body Paragraph
   a. Topic sentence (What will you cover in this paragraph?)
   b. Background information about this topic
   c. Details from your research
   d. Explanation of what the details mean and why they're significant
   e. Concluding sentence that restates the topic sentence

5. Concluding Paragraph
   a. Restate the thesis statement
   b. Summarize your findings
   c. Restate the purpose/tell readers how this research can be used

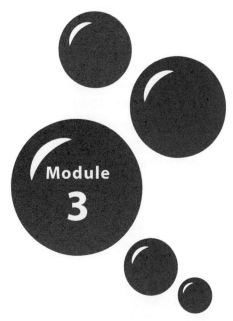

GUIDED EXPERIMENTATION

Objectives

Students will learn, review, and practice the scientific method while having a chance to get hands-on STEM experience that supports and motivates their upcoming design module.

Overview

This hands-on module will make the learning more real and relevant, especially for kinesthetic learners. But it doesn't have to be elaborate! The materials used are the kind that can be found around the house—plastic bottles, cups, paper, etc. Even if time/resources only permit a single experiment station, students will still be able to go through the scientific process of asking a question, formulating a hypothesis, observing results, and drawing conclusions. They'll also get to see the properties of water and air for themselves and develop a deeper interest and connection with the subject matter.

All classes should complete Mini-Lesson 3.1 and Mini-Lesson 3.2 for grounding in forming hypotheses and understanding quantitative and qualitative results. Afterward, lead the class in a short discussion on the responsible and safe ways to use class resources while conducting experiments. The takeaway from your conversation should be about conserving materials by only taking what you need and reusing materials whenever possible. Your class should perform one to all of the experiments.

 DOI: 10.4324/9781003233831-6

Tech Connections

Take photos and short videos (5–30 seconds) of the experiments, and post them on the classroom Twitter, Instagram, and/or Facebook pages with the hashtag #couldyouliveunderwater. Make sure to take plenty of photos that can also be utilized in student blog posts.

Writing Connections

There are suggested journal entries and suggested blog posts in the Concluding Activities section. For classrooms keeping a blog, encourage students to use the provided blog post titles as inspiration for what they will write.

Time Frame

Time Period	One Class Period (45–90 min.)	One Extended Period (90–120 min.)	One Week (5 Class Periods)
Activities	• Mini-Lesson 3.1: What Will Happen?: A Guide to Forming a Hypothesis • Mini-Lesson 3.2: What Happened?: A Guide to Quantitative and Qualitative Observation • Conduct 2–3 experiments (see Handouts 3.3–3.8) • Discuss results	• Mini-Lesson 3.1: What Will Happen?: A Guide to Forming a Hypothesis • Mini-Lesson 3.2: What Happened?: A Guide to Quantitative and Qualitative Observation • Conduct 4–6 experiments (see Handouts 3.3–3.8) • Discuss results	• Mini-Lesson 3.1: What Will Happen?: A Guide to Forming a Hypothesis • Mini-Lesson 3.2: What Happened?: A Guide to Quantitative and Qualitative Observation • Conduct 4–6 experiments (see Handouts 3.3–3.8) • Discuss results • Create class posters

One Class Period: After completing Mini-Lessons 3.1 and 3.2, the teacher takes the class through two or three experiments using one set of materials for each. Following along on the corresponding handout(s), students give their hypotheses out loud, note their observations, and discuss the results all together.

One Extended Class Period: After completing Mini-Lessons 3.1 and 3.2, the teacher takes the class through 4–6 of the experiments using one set of materials. Using the corresponding handout(s), students give their hypotheses out loud, note their observations, and discuss the results all together. Alternatively, students work in small groups to each conduct one experiment. Each group writes down its hypothesis, observations, and results. Each group shares its results.

One Week: After completing Mini-Lessons 3.1 and 3.2, students work in groups or individually to conduct 4–6 of the experiments. Students write down their hypotheses, their observations, and their results using the corresponding handouts. Results are shared, and the entire class discusses them. Experiments are at six different stations, and students rotate through them. At each station, students formulate a hypothesis, write down/draw their observations, and state their results. They might also be prompted to pose questions that they will bring to the discussion on Day 5.

- **Day 1:** Teacher presents the steps of the scientific method. Class completes Mini-Lesson 3.1: What Will Happen?: A Guide to Forming a Hypothesis and Mini-Lesson 3.2: What Happened?: A Guide to Quantitative and Qualitative Observation.
- **Day 2:** Students rotate through the experiment stations as teacher circulates.
- **Day 3:** Students rotate through the experiment stations as teacher circulates.
- **Day 4:** Sharing of results and class discussion.
- **Day 5:** Scientific poster creation. Concluding Activities.

WHAT WILL HAPPEN?: A GUIDE TO FORMING A HYPOTHESIS

Suggested Materials

- Student copies of Handout 3.1: What Will Happen?: A Guide to Forming a Hypothesis

Sequence

1. Open this lesson by explaining what a hypothesis is and how it's used. Distribute Handout 3.1: What Will Happen?: A Guide to Forming a Hypothesis. Share examples of well-crafted hypotheses.

2. Draw parallels between creating a hypothesis and defining a problem (Module 1). Explain how when a hypothesis is proven wrong, scientists then know what doesn't work, and that's very valuable information when looking for solutions to problems. Compare: Both are specific and testable. Contrast: A hypothesis is a statement. A defined problem is a question.

3. Walk students through examples of well- and poorly crafted hypotheses. Ask: *Are these hypotheses specific? Testable? Do they focus on only one variable?*
   o Examples of well-crafted hypotheses:
      - If I put a piece of paper inside a glass jar, and then submerge the jar underwater, the paper will get wet.
      - If I dissolve salt into water, the freezing point will decrease.

   o Examples of poorly crafted hypotheses:
      - Water is good at dissolving salt.
      - It's easier to see underwater with a viewer.

Mini-Lesson 3.2

WHAT HAPPENED?: A GUIDE TO QUANTITATIVE AND QUALITATIVE OBSERVATION

Suggested Materials

- Student Design Notebooks
- Student copies of Handout 3.2: What Happened?: A Guide to Quantitative and Qualitative Observation

Sequence

1. Tell students that when they conduct their experiments later in this module, they'll be asked to predict whether their results will be *qualitative* or *quantitative*. Their ability to observe qualitative changes will be very important in Module 5 when they test the prototypes they will make. Encourage them to practice and strengthen these skills now.
2. Begin with a class discussion on the difference between quantitative and qualitative observations and data collections. First, share the definitions of each, and then use the examples on Handout 3.2 to differentiate between the two.
3. Create a large two-column chart where the class can see it (see Figure 2). Use the graphic organizer to differentiate between qualitative and quantitative observations and sort examples of each.

QUANTITATIVE VERSUS QUALITATIVE OBSERVATIONS

Quantitative Data	Qualitative Data
The temperature of the mixture was raised by 5 degrees Celsius.	The color changed from dark red to light red.

Figure 2. Two-column chart example.

GUIDED EXPERIMENTATION

Suggested Materials

- Video: "Underwater During Hurricane Gonzalo" (for Experiment 5, available at https://www.youtube.com/watch?v=i5rJ5y8ngtw)
- Experiment materials (see Handouts 3.3–3.8)
- Student Design Notebooks
- Student copies of teacher-selected experiment handouts (Handouts 3.3–3.8)

Preparation

Before teaching this module, choose how many and which experiments you want your class to complete. Gather your experiment materials, and create individual stations for each experiment in your classroom.

Sequence

1. Introduce your students to each experiment. Explain that they will have an opportunity to investigate the properties of water and practice crafting hypotheses and differentiating between quantitative and qualitative results. All of this information should inform how they design and test their prototypes in Modules 4 and 5.
2. Distribute handouts for each experiment.
3. Circulate around the class to offer support as students complete experiments individually or as small groups.

CONCLUDING ACTIVITIES

Journal Prompts for Student Reflection

- Which experiments do you think will inform your design the most? Why?
- What did you find challenging about conducting these experiments?
- The next time you conduct experiments, what would you like to do differently?
- Would anything have made the experimentation process easier or more effective for you?
- What advice would you give to someone else who is about to start experimenting with water?

Suggested Assignments

- Thoughtfully respond to any three of the journal prompts; include these in your Design Notebook.
- Continue experimentation.
- Create a poster to share the results of one or more of your experiments.

Suggested Blog Posts

- A Beginner's Guide to the Scientific Method
- 3 Surprising Ways You're Using the Scientific Method in Your Everyday Life
- Quantitative Versus Qualitative Data: What's the Difference?
- Top 10 Ways to Save Water at Home and at School
- Behind the Scenes of [Name of Experiment]
- 5 Tips for Making a Memorable Poster

Handout 3.1
What Will Happen?: A Guide to Forming a Hypothesis

Directions: A hypothesis is often described as an "educated guess." It's a prediction about the answer to a question, and it's based on prior experience and research. Each hypothesis you create will need to be specific, testable, and focus on only one variable. Use the following tips to guide you in formulating a hypothesis.

1. **Is it specific?** Did you include words like *good* or *bad* in your hypothesis? These words are too vague to be useful. Instead try words like *increase, decrease,* or *change color*.

2. **Is it testable?** Are you able to create an experiment to test your hypothesis given your time, experience, and resources? If the answer is yes, you've got a testable hypothesis on your hands.

3. **Is the focus on only one variable?** Variables are the parameters of an experiment that can be measured and changed. Aspects like temperature, color, and mass are all considered variables.

4. When performing experiments try using this writing frame to create your hypothesis: *If I do _____, then _____ will happen.*

5. Remember that when a hypothesis is wrong, it does not reflect poorly on the scientists. Disproven hypotheses are very useful when performing research. Before we can know what does work, we first must find out what doesn't.

Handout 3.2

What Happened?: A Guide to Quantitative and Qualitative Observation

Directions: Observing your experiments and gathering results either *quantitatively* or *qualitatively* is how you will evaluate if your hypothesis is correct or incorrect. Quantitative evaluation is specific and measurable. It tells us how much or how little of something happened, along with measurements. In other words, quantitative data focuses on quantities. Qualitative observations, on the other hand, focus on qualities of your research that cannot be measured but can be observed with your senses.

Below is list of observations. Determine whether each observation is qualitative or quantitative. Circle your response.

1. The color changed from light red to dark red.   Qualitative   Quantitative

2. The temperature increased 5 degrees Celsius.   Qualitative   Quantitative

3. The mixture got colder.   Qualitative   Quantitative

4. A strong smell was detected.   Qualitative   Quantitative

5. A blue flame was observed.   Qualitative   Quantitative

Now create a few observations of your own. Are they qualitative or quantitative?

6. _____   Qualitative   Quantitative

   _____

   _____

7. _____   Qualitative   Quantitative

   _____

   _____

8. _____   Qualitative   Quantitative

   _____

   _____

Handout 3.3

Experiment 1: Is it Possible to Keep a Piece of Paper Dry Underwater?

Hypothesis

1. What is your hypothesis?

2. Will your results be qualitative or quantitative?

Materials

- Large container
- Water (enough to fill the container so the glass can be completely submerged)
- Clear glass
- Paper towel

Procedure

1. Fill your container with enough water to submerge your glass vertically.
2. Ball up the paper towel and push it down into the very bottom of the glass until it stays lodged when you turn the glass upside down.
3. With the glass upside down, and the paper towel securely in place, use your hand to submerge the glass until it is completely underwater. Be careful not to tip the glass; keep it as vertical as possible as you dunk and then lift the glass from underwater.
4. Now inspect the paper towel. Did it get wet?

Handout 3.3, Continued.

Discussion Questions

Directions: After completing the experiment, answer the following questions.

1. Did the paper towel get wet? Why do you think it did or didn't?

2. As you submerge the glass, the water pushes the air into the glass. The air inside the glass is compressed, and the air pressure inside the glass increases. This pressure increase prevents water from entering into the glass and touching the paper towel. How might this information be useful as you design your underwater city prototype?

Handout 3.4

Experiment 2: Can a Paper Clip Float on Top of Water?

Hypothesis

1. What is your hypothesis?

2. Will your results be qualitative or quantitative?

Materials

- Small paper clips (size #1 work best)
- Small opaque cup or bowl
- Water

Procedure

1. Fill your cup or bowl with water.
2. Drop a few paper clips into the water and allow them to sink; this proves that paper clips are denser than water.
3. Carefully float another paper clip on the surface of water. Try using your fingers to do this. If you have difficulty, you can unbend another paper clip and use it as makeshift tweezers to assist you.
4. Is the paper clip floating?

Handout 3.4, Continued.

Discussion Questions

Directions: After completing the experiment, answer the following questions.

1. Why does a paper clip float on the surface of water, even though paper clips are more dense than water?

2. Water molecules are pulled together by a force called cohesion. This is why water forms droplets and why those water droplets combine with each other to make little streams of water like in a rainstorm. This cohesion creates a phenomenon in water called surface tension. Due to cohesion, water molecules form a strong "skin" or a tension on the surface of water that allows some objects to float, despite their difference in density. How might this information be useful as you design your underwater city prototype?

Handout 3.5

Experiment 3: Is It Possible to See Underwater?

Hypothesis

1. What is your hypothesis?

2. Will your results be qualitative or quantitative?

Materials

- Plastic half-gallon milk jug
- Craft knife
- Clear plastic wrap
- Heavy-duty rubber band
- Large container
- Water (enough to fill the container about 25 centimeters deep)
- Coin

Procedure

1. Place the coin in the container of water.
2. Carefully cut away the top of the half-gallon milk jug, leaving the handle.
3. Cut away the bottom of the jug.
4. Cut a piece of the clear plastic wrap large enough to cover the bottom of the milk jug. Stretch the plastic wrap over the bottom of the milk jug and secure it with the heavy rubber band. This becomes your viewer.
5. Submerge the viewer in water while holding on to the handle. Look through the top of the jug. What do you see?

Handout 3.5, Continued.

Discussion Questions

Directions: After completing the experiment, answer the following questions.

1. Does the apparatus you made help you to see underwater? If so, how do you think it works? Can you see the coin? If so, how does it appear?

2. Light travels through transparent substances at different rates depending on what that substance is. This means that light travels differently through the air, water, and glass. This is one reason why underwater objects look magnified through your viewer. How could this information affect how we build and live underwater?

Handout 3.6

Experiment 4: Does Salt Concentration Affect the Density of Water?

Hypothesis

1. What is your hypothesis?

2. Will your results be qualitative or quantitative?

Materials

- Table salt
- Warm water
- Teaspoon
- 6 different colors of food coloring
- Clear plastic straws
- 6 clear plastic cups

Procedure

1. Using six clear plastic cups, place one teaspoon of salt in the first cup, two teaspoons in the second, three teaspoons in the third, four in the fourth, five in the fifth, and six in the sixth.
2. Fill each cup with the same amount of warm water.
3. Stir each cup until the salt has dissolved.
4. Add 3–4 drops of food coloring to each cup. Use a different color for each cup.
5. Take a clear straw and dip it into the solution with the least amount of salt about one inch, and then place your thumb over the top of the straw to trap the liquid inside.
6. Keep your thumb over the straw and dip the straw into the cup with the second least amount of salt about 2 inches in. Take your thumb off, and then place it back on the top of the straw.
7. Continue in this manner, each time dipping the straw in the next most concentrated salt solution and 1 inch deeper.
8. After you've added each solution to your straw, what do you see? There should be a tower of colors, clearly defined like a rainbow.
9. Now, using a clean straw, try adding the solutions to your straw in the reverse order, and then try mixing them up by shaking the straw. What happens?

Handout 3.6, Continued.

Discussion Questions

Directions: After completing the experiment, answer the following questions.

1. Do you think the different concentrations of salt affected how the solutions stacked inside your straw? Why or why not?

2. A solution's density is formulated by determining the mass of a substance relative to its volume. As you increased the amount of salt in your cups of water, you also increased the density of your salt solutions. The solution with the most salt is the densest and is therefore the heaviest. This is why the solution with the most salt stayed at the bottom of your straw. This is also why the solution with the least amount of salt stays at the top of your straw; it is the lightest. How might this information factor into how you build your underwater living prototype?

Handout 3.7
Experiment 5: Build an Underwater Storm Simulator

Hypothesis

1. What is your hypothesis?

2. Will your results be qualitative or quantitative?

Materials

- 2 clear, identical plastic bottles (2-liter soft drink bottles work well)
- One metal washer the size of the bottle opening
- Duct tape
- Water
- Baby oil
- Small plastic beads
- Food coloring

Resource

- "Underwater During Hurricane Gonzalo" (available at https://www.youtube.com/watch?v=i5rJ5y8ngtw)

Procedure

1. Fill one bottle three-fourths with water.
2. Add food coloring to the water.
3. Place the metal washer on top of the mouth of the bottle.
4. Invert the second bottle onto the first bottle.
5. Duct-tape the two bottles together tightly to create a seal so no liquid comes out.
6. Invert the entire apparatus and swirl it gently to create a vortex of colored water inside the bottles. You've created an underwater storm stimulator.
7. Try creating another storm simulator, but this time add beads to the water, or try creating one with oil and water. How are they different from each other?

Handout 3.7, Continued.

Discussion Questions

Directions: After completing the experiment, answer the following questions.

1. In what ways did you accurately recreate an underwater storm?

2. How do you think underwater storms will affect humans' ability to build and live underwater?

Handout 3.8

Experiment 6: What Is Water Made of?

Hypothesis

1. What is your hypothesis?

2. Will your results be qualitative or quantitative?

Materials

*   2 pencils, sharpened on both ends
*   2 double-sided alligator clips with connecting wire
*   9-volt battery
*   Electrical tape
*   Clear plastic cup
*   Water
*   Salt

Procedure

1. Place both pencils on either side of the battery, parallel to each other.
2. Wrap the pencils and battery with electrical tape to hold them in that position.
3. Connect one lead from each wire to one tip of each pencil.
4. Connect the other leads from the wires to the battery terminals.
5. Fill the cup three-fourths with water. Add a pinch of salt.
6. Take the tips of the pencils not connected with wires to the battery and submerge them in the water, without touching the sides or the bottom.
7. Observe the pencils in the water for 1–2 minutes. What do you see?

Handout 3.8, Continued.

Discussion Questions

Directions: After completing the experiment, answer the following questions.

1. If you saw bubbles, did you notice that one pencil had twice as many bubbles as the other? Why may that be?

2. One water molecule is made up of two hydrogen atoms bound to an oxygen atom. When you electrified the water, you broke the bonds of a water molecule, resulting in hydrogen atoms and oxygen atoms being released in the form of gas. There are two hydrogen atoms for every one oxygen atom. That is why there are twice as many bubbles on one of your pencils. If you can use electricity to break water up into hydrogen and oxygen gas, what does that mean for designing underwater habitats?

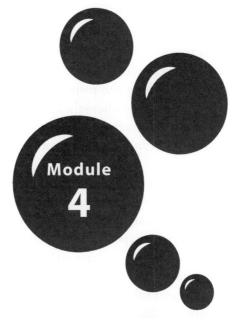

DESIGNING AND BUILDING PROTOTYPES

Objectives

In this module, students will use the knowledge and understanding gained through the research and ideating phases to build their own prototypes using household materials.

Overview

This hands-on module is a powerful chance for students to apply what they've learned from their research and make the learning more real and relevant, especially for kinesthetic learners. In addition, this module immerses students in a positive atmosphere of iterating and solving problems as they arise, giving them a chance to build resilience and enjoy growth.

As with the experiments in Module 3, the building in Module 4 need not be elaborate to be effective. The materials used for building are the kind that can be found around the house—plastic bottles, paper towel tubes, tinfoil, tape, etc. A list of suggested materials is provided on page 10 so that teachers can plan ahead and enlist the help of parents and volunteers in gathering materials.

***Teacher's Note*. Creating a design atmosphere.** For this module, it's vital to remind students of where they are in the design thinking process by having them check back in with their design thinking posters. This is the time to try, be experimental, take notice of what's working, test, collaborate, and use their creativity to problem solve.

 DOI: 10.4324/9781003233831-7

As students design and build prototypes, invite them to enjoy the process of iteration. They may try ideas they're really excited about, only to see those ideas not turn out the way they expected. That is wonderful! The core of design thinking is observing what's working and responding to what isn't. Remind students about the experimentation stage where they learned that an incorrect hypothesis still brings scientists closer to understanding the truth. The same thing occurs in design: A prototype that doesn't work brings students closer to figuring out what does work.

The atmosphere of the learning space during this phase should be electric. It should be buzzing with students' excitement and ingenuity. Your role in creating this atmosphere is key. You can help learners to remember that success does not mean getting a working prototype on the first try; it means continuing to design and refine in order to address the surprises that arise. Think about how your language can help the students to embrace a trial-and-error mindset:

- "Wow, what a great solution you found!"
- "I'm so impressed that you thought to do that."
- "I see that you're really thinking through this problem. Way to go!"
- "Look at all of the different ways we've come up with of addressing the issue of [   ]!"
- "I love all of the determination I'm seeing as I look at the designing going on in here!"

Tech Connections

Designs and prototypes can be photographed and shared on a classroom or school website or social media page. Using the hashtag #couldyouliveunderwater, classes will be able to search for results from other classes and schools. Consider taking pictures and short (5- to 30-second) videos of the design process in your classroom for use on your classroom blog or social media pages.

Encourage students to generate questions they would want to ask professional designers and engineers. Using the classroom Twitter account and/or Instagram account, follow some prominent people in the fields of design and engineering. Favorite and comment on their posts in order to start a conversation, and then post student questions to see if you can get responses. Share the responses with the class and encourage students to come up with follow-up questions or "thank you" posts.

Writing Connections

There are suggested journal entries and suggested blog posts in the Concluding Activities section. For classrooms keeping a blog, encourage students to use the provided blog post titles as inspiration for what they will write.

Time Frame

Time Period	One Class Period (45–90 min.)	One Extended Period (90–120 min.)	One Week (5 Class Periods)
Activities	• Mini-Lesson 4.1: Challenges, Needs, Advantages, and Opportunities of Designing Underwater • Mini-Lesson 4.2: What Will It Do in Saltwater? • Design and build prototypes	• Mini-Lesson 4.1: Challenges, Needs, Advantages, and Opportunities of Designing Underwater • Mini-Lesson 4.2: What Will It Do in Saltwater? • Mini-Lesson 4.3: Guidelines for Designing • Build prototypes	• Mini-Lesson 4.1: Challenges, Needs, Advantages, and Opportunities of Designing Underwater • Mini-Lesson 4.2: What Will It Do in Saltwater? • Mini-Lesson 4.3: Guidelines for Designing • Build prototypes • Concluding Activities

One Class Period: The class reviews the lessons and conclusions from the Research and Experiment phases and completes Mini-Lesson 4.1: Challenges, Needs, Advantages, and Opportunities so that students are primed for smart designing. The teacher presents Mini-Lesson 4.2: What Will It Do in Saltwater? Students begin designing on paper, determining both what they will build and the procedure they will use to build it. The class decides on a single design to build so that students have the maximum support from the teacher and each other. Students work in groups to determine a procedure and to build the prototype using materials that have been gathered in advance.

One Extended Period: The class reviews the lessons and conclusions from the Research and Experiment phases and completes Mini-Lesson 4.1: Challenges, Needs, Advantages, and Opportunities so that students are primed for smart designing. The teacher presents Mini-Lesson 4.2: What Will It Do in Saltwater? The teacher presents Mini-Lesson 4.3: Guidelines for Designing. Students begin designing on paper, determining both what they will build and the procedure they will use to build it. The class decides on a single design to build so that students have the maximum support from the teacher and each other. Students work individually or in groups to outline their procedure and to build the prototype using materials that have been gathered in advance. Alternatively, each student decides on his or her own design to build and outlines the procedure. Prototypes are built using materials that have been gathered in advance. Alternatively, students work in small groups to design and build a prototype of their choosing and determine their procedure. Prototypes are built using materials that have been gathered in advance.

One Week: Students work in groups or individually to design and build their prototypes.

- **Day 1:** The class reviews the lessons and conclusions from the Research and Experiment phases and completes Mini-Lesson 4.1: Challenges, Needs, Advantages, and Opportunities. This could occur via a class discussion, or by having students make posters that list underwater challenges, needs, advantages, and opportunities, so that they are primed for smart designing. Students begin designing on paper, determining both what they will build and the procedure they will use to build it.
- **Day 2:** The class discusses the materials available, and the teacher presents Mini-Lesson 4.2: What Will It Do in Saltwater? and Mini-Lesson 4.3: Guidelines for Designing. Students continue designing and begin building, as the teacher circulates to check in.
- **Day 3:** Students continue working on their prototypes or reiterate their designs as needed.
- **Day 4:** Students continue working on their prototypes or reiterate their designs as needed.
- **Day 5:** Students finish building their prototypes and may decorate them if time permits, add on to their designs, modify them, help other groups, or whatever best facilitates all students finishing prototypes. Students self-evaluate using Handout 4.5: Self-Evaluation Questions. Students complete Concluding Activities.

Mini-Lesson 4.1

CHALLENGES, NEEDS, ADVANTAGES, AND OPPORTUNITIES OF DESIGNING UNDERWATER

Suggested Materials

- Research reports or notes from Module 2 (for reference)
- Completed Handouts 3.3–3.8 (whichever handouts were completed corresponding to the experiments in Module 3)
- Lined and unlined paper for brainstorming
- Student Design Notebooks
- Handout 4.1: Sample Thought Organizers
- Handout 4.2: Challenges, Needs, Advantages, and Opportunities of Designing Underwater

Sequence

1. Tell students that, as a class, you will be working to understand the challenges of designing and building underwater, as well as its advantages. Let them know that the goal will be to take the challenges and advantages of the underwater environment and examine them one at a time. For each challenge, students should work to come up with a corresponding need, and for each advantage they should come up with a corresponding opportunity.

2. Draw two tables on the board, modeled from Figure 3. Leave the tables blank except for the headings "Challenges," "Needs," Advantages," and "Opportunities," and add the following to the first row of the first column of the Challenges and Needs table: "People can't breathe/live in water."

3. Tell students that they will be using what they learned from the research they completed in Module 2 and the experiments in Module 3 to understand the challenges and advantages of designing underwater. Distribute Handout 4.1: Sample Thought Organizers and Handout 4.2: Challenges, Needs, Advantages, and Opportunities of Designing Underwater. Demonstrate to students how to place some of the ideas from the graphic organizers on Handout 4.1 into the table on Handout 4.2, so that they see how to organize the ideas.

4. Explain to students that the mind map and the idea chain are both ways of brainstorming and organizing ideas. Tell them that mind maps provide space for several different related ideas and are very effective for some kinds of thinkers. Idea chains provide step-by-step frameworks for

Challenges	Corresponding Needs
People can't breathe/live in water.	Structure must be reliably watertight.
Salt water corrodes some materials.	Materials that don't corrode in saltwater.
Great pressure can crush things.	Equal and opposite pressure.
People can't breathe/live in water.	Valves and pumps for points of ingress/egress.

Advantages	Corresponding Opportunities
Water is made up of hydrogen and oxygen atoms.	Oxygen is necessary for people to breathe.
Saltwater is conductive.	Use water for electricity.
Current has kinetic energy.	Use water for electricity.
People need water, and there will be a lot of it around!	Use water desalination to turn seawater into potable water.

Figure 3. Sample challenges, needs, advantages, and opportunities.

listing effects, results, or consequences, and they are very helpful for other kinds of thinkers. Instruct students to use either type of thought organizer or their own brainstorming methods to write down their own ideas about the challenges, needs, advantages, and opportunities of building underwater and then add them to Handout 4.2. This can be done as a class, in pairs, or in small groups. If desired, provide them with additional examples from Figure 3.

5. As students work, guide and support them with leading questions based on Figure 3 to help lead them to conclusions that will help them with the design stage.

Mini-Lesson 4.2

WHAT WILL IT DO IN SALTWATER?

Suggested Materials

- Student Design Notebooks
- Student copies of Handout 4.3: What Will It Do in Saltwater?
- Materials for student prototypes (see p. 10)

Sequence

1. Distribute Handout 4. 3: What Will It Do in Saltwater? Working as a class or in small groups, students can fill out their predictions about each material your class is using to build prototypes. This is also a way for you to introduce which materials are available so that students can design with them in mind. We recommend having the materials out so that students can see them and consider them more thoughtfully as they make their predictions.

2. Remind students what they learned in the experimental phase about density and surface tension. Discuss the differences between freshwater and saltwater. What changes when the water contains salt? Why?

3. Remind them also about forming a hypothesis, an educated guess. Students will use their best thinking to predict what each material will do, but they won't know for certain how their prototypes will behave until they test them. That's the point of the prototypes!

4. Simply asking "why" following each student prediction about the behavior of a material is an effective way to gauge whether students are applying what they have learned from other modules and are engaging with the process of design thinking. Remain neutral to student answers; remember, the feedback will come naturally from the prototype-testing stage. Simply acknowledge that students are explaining their predictions clearly or are using their reasoning to draw conclusions. There's no need to correct false assumptions.

GUIDELINES FOR DESIGNING

Suggested Materials

- Unlined paper for designing
- Crayons, colored pencils, or other art supplies for making a color-coded legend
- Materials for student prototypes (see p. 10)
- Student Design Notebooks with completed student copies of Handouts 4.2–4.3
- Handout 4.4: My Prototype Checklist

Sequence

1. Get students excited: They're about to start designing prototypes! This is the perfect time to remind them of where they are in the design thinking process and to introduce or reinforce the ideas in the Teacher's Note about creating a design atmosphere (pp. 95–96).
2. If not working together as a class, divide students into design teams. Ask each student to have Handouts 4.2 and 4.3 handy or accessible in his or her Design Notebook.
3. Distribute Handout 4.4: My Prototype Checklist, and instruct each student/design team to fill it out using the information from Handout 4.2 and 4.3.
4. Once students have completed Handout 4.4, begin a discussion about prototypes. Help students see that their prototypes are like dioramas or models in that they won't function in the same way as what they represent; instead, the prototypes will provide a way for students to gain a greater understanding of what they could expect were they to build their designs in reality.
5. Instruct students to begin designing their prototypes, drawing the structures they will build. Their drawings can be anything from rough sketches to scale plans, depending on the skill level of and time available to your class. Instruct students to include labels in their designs (e.g., equipment storage room, mess hall, water filtration station, recreation room, etc.). Emphasize that students should spend time thinking through their designs, as this is an important way to preserve and protect resources by using them with intention.
6. Once they have drawn their designs, students should be encouraged to think through which materials they will use and to create a legend showing which materials will be used where. This can be done with colored pencils, crayons, markers, or any other art materials on hand in the classroom.

CONCLUDING ACTIVITIES

Journal Prompts for Student Reflection

- What did you enjoy about designing and building your prototype?
- What did you find challenging about designing and building your prototype?
- The next time you design or build, what would you like to do differently?
- Would anything have made the designing and building process easier or more effective for you?
- What advice would you give to someone else who is about to design and build a prototype?

Suggested Assignments

- Evaluate your work on this module using Handout 4.5: Self-Evaluation Questions.
- Thoughtfully respond to any three of the journal prompts; include these in your Design Notebook.
- Polish your design drawing to share with the class and include in your Design Notebook.
- Create an artist's rendering—a drawing, painting, collage, or graphic design—to help viewers imagine how your prototype will be used.

Suggested Blog Posts

- How to Think Like a Designer
- The 10 Best Materials for Building Prototypes
- What I Learned by Designing a Prototype
- A Tour of My Design From Top to Bottom
- Design Mindset: How to Think and Build Like an Engineer

Handout 4.1

Sample Thought Organizers

Directions: Below you will see two different ways of organizing ideas: a mind map and an idea chain. Read through each graphic organizer. Notice how one idea flows to the next. Ask yourself how the ideas are connected. Can you imagine using one of these types of brainstorming activities to organize your own thoughts?

Mind Map

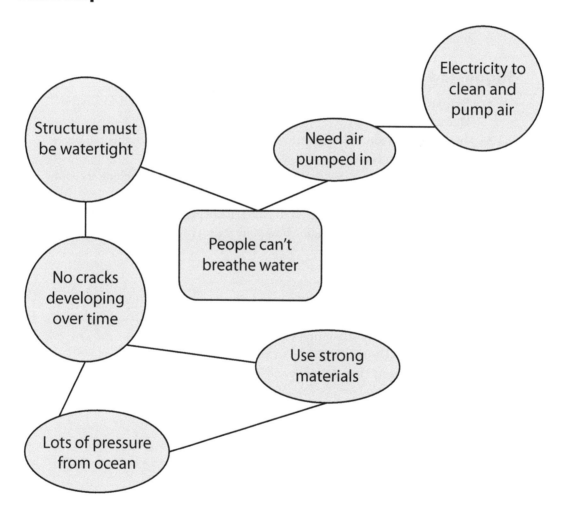

Idea Chain

people will drown in water → structure must be watertight → people will suffocate in an airtight structure → air must be pumped in on a continuous basis → having air tanks would be hard to sustain → need a way to clean the carbon dioxide out of the air

Handout 4.2

Challenges, Needs, Advantages, and
Opportunities of Designing Underwater

Directions: There are both challenges and advantages to designing a livable underwater habitat. Complete the two charts. The first chart asks you to describe the challenges of living underwater, and then to think of what kind of solution would address each challenge. The second chart asks you to think of the advantages of building underwater, and then to think of the opportunities they provide. A few examples have been provided.

Get creative! What kinds of neat innovations could you use when building underwater that would not be available on land? Think about the guided experiment(s) you conducted in Module 3 and what you learned about density, pressure, and the component parts of water. Use Handout 4.1 to help you think of challenges, needs, advantages, and opportunities.

Challenges and Needs

Challenge	Corresponding Need
People can't breathe/live in water.	People need a source of breathable air.
Salt water corrodes some materials.	
Great pressure can crush things.	
People can't breathe/live in water.	

COULD YOU LIVE UNDERWATER? © Taylor & Francis Group

Handout 4.2, Continued.

Advantages and Opportunities

Advantage	Corresponding Opportunity
Water is made of hydrogen and oxygen atoms.	*The oxygen could be repurposed.*
Saltwater is conductive.	
Current has kinetic energy.	
People need water, and there will be a lot of it around!	

Handout 4.3

What Will It Do in Salt Water?

Directions: Look at each material your teacher has provided for your prototype. Make a prediction about how it will behave when placed in saltwater. Use the list of suggested actions to help you.

Material	What Will It Do in Saltwater?

Suggested Actions

float on the surface	lose its seal
sink to the bottom	remain sticky
float partway down to the bottom	lose its stickiness
disintegrate	crumble
keep water in/out	fill with water
form a seal	

Handout 4.4
My Prototype Checklist

Directions: Using what you learned in the Challenges, Needs, Advantages, and Opportunities activity, you can create a list of the elements your design will have. For example, how will you keep your structure stable? Will it float? If so, how? Will it rest on the bottom of the sea? If so, what will it need to do that? How will people get air? How will you address waste and freshwater needs?

Use your completed Handout 4.2 to make a list of all the elements you want to include in your prototype. Your list should be based on the "Needs" column and the "Opportunities" column of Handout 4.2.

My Prototype Will Have . . .

Handout 4.5
Self-Evaluation Questions

Directions: Use these questions to think about the design process you just completed. There are no right or wrong answers; simply reflect on your experience and write what is true for you.

1. What did you enjoy about designing and building your prototype?

2. What did you find challenging about designing and building your prototype?

3. What is something you're proud of that you did in this module? Did you solve a tough problem? Did you help someone else solve a problem? Did you keep going when things got hard or frustrating? Were you flexible and adaptive?

4. What was your design process? Describe the steps you took to build your prototype.

Handout 4.5, Continued.

5. The next time you design and build, what would you like to do differently?

6. Would anything have made the designing and building process easier or more effective for you?

7. What advice would you give to someone else who is about to start designing or building a prototype?

Testing Prototypes

Objectives

Students will understand how to select criteria for testing their prototypes. They will also build resilience by experiencing firsthand the recursive and iterative nature of the design process.

Overview

In this module, students will test their underwater habitat prototypes under controlled conditions and evaluate them based on specified criteria. Depending on the time available, classes can use predetermined testing criteria or generate and decide on their own. If using predetermined testing criteria, the teacher will need to decide on these prior to presenting the lesson. This can be done by reading through Mini-Lesson 5:1: Evaluation Criteria.

Tech Connections

Testing the prototypes can be filmed and shared on a classroom or school website or social media page, using the hashtag #couldyouliveunderwater. Classes will be able to search for results from other classes and schools. Viewing other prototypes will help to instill the lesson that there is no single correct answer to real-life design problems.

 DOI: 10.4324/9781003233831-8

Writing Connections

There are suggested journal entries and suggested blog posts in the Concluding Activities section. For classrooms keeping a blog, encourage students to use the provided blog post titles as inspiration for what they will write.

Time Frame

Time Period	One Class Period (45–90 min.)	One Extended Period (90–120 min.)	One Week (5 Class Periods)
Activities	• Teacher presents testing criteria determined prior to start of lesson • Test prototypes • Discuss results	• Mini-Lesson 5.1: Evaluation Criteria • Test prototypes using Handout 5.1: Design Evaluation Data • Discuss results	• Mini-Lesson 5.1: Evaluation Criteria • Short-test prototypes using Handout 5.1: Design Evaluation Data • Long-test prototypes using Handout 5.1: Design Evaluation Data • Mini-Lesson 5.2: A Guide to Constructive Evaluation • Discuss results • Concluding Activities

One Class Period: The teacher presents the evaluation criteria, and each prototype is tested and observed. Students use Handout 5.1: Design Evaluation Data to note the criteria met by each prototype, or they work together to fill in a group evaluation table on the board. Class discussion follows.

One Extended Period: The teacher presents the evaluation criteria or presents Mini-Lesson 5.1: Evaluation Criteria. Each prototype is tested and observed. Students use Handout 5.1: Design Evaluation Data chart to note the criteria met by each prototype, or they work together to fill in a group evaluation table on the board. Class discussion follows.

One Week: The teacher presents Mini-Lesson 5.1: Evaluation Criteria. Students generate the criteria for evaluation and then test their prototypes. With the additional time available, students can both short- and long-test their prototypes by completing an initial test (1–5 minutes), and then completing longer tests of 15 minutes or up to one hour. The teacher presents Mini-Lesson 5.2: A Guide to Constructive Evaluation before guiding the students in a discussion about what was learned during the testing phase.

- **Day 1:** The teacher presents Mini-Lesson 5.1: Evaluation Criteria. During a class discussion, students decide on the evaluation criteria, prompted by the teacher and helped by their problem statements from Module 1.

They then fill in their chosen criteria on Handout 5:1 Design Evaluation Data. Prototype testing and evaluation begins, using the Design Evaluation Data charts.

- **Day 2:** Prototype testing and evaluation continues, using the Design Evaluation Data charts.
- **Day 3:** Prototype testing and evaluation continues, using the Design Evaluation Data charts.
- **Day 4:** Prototype testing and evaluation continues, using the Design Evaluation Data charts.
- **Day 5:** Prototype testing and evaluation finishes, using the Design Evaluation Data charts. (Plan for fewer tests on this day.) The teacher presents Mini-Lesson 5.2: A Guide to Constructive Evaluation. Class discussion follows. Concluding Activities.

EVALUATION CRITERIA

Suggested Materials

- Student Design Notebooks
- Student copies of Handout 5.1: Design Evaluation Data

Sequence

1. Ask: *How will you evaluate your design for living underwater?* Remind students that a prototype isn't designed to behave exactly like the real thing; instead, it provides an opportunity to view the design in physical space and get a preview of how it would behave. A prototype is an idea made three-dimensional.

2. Whether the students are deciding on their own evaluation criteria or using criteria supplied or guided by the teacher, the class should begin by discussing what general criteria will be useful for evaluating prototypes.

3. Before creating evaluation criteria, ask students to go back to the problem they defined in Module 1 and the hypothesis they created in Module 3. Ask students how that information might affect the evaluation criteria they choose. Will the tests result in qualitative or quantitative data? Regardless, all evaluation criteria must result in an easy-to-observe and understandable result.

4. Questions for creating criteria include:
   o Remaining in place: Does it float up? Does it tip over? Does it get pushed by the current?
   o Structural integrity: Does it collapse? How does water affect the structure?
   o Watertightness: Does it leak? Does it become waterlogged?
   o Effects of time: How does it hold up over 5 minutes? 15 minutes? 1 hour?

5. Students may use Handout 5.1: Design Evaluation Data to record the evaluation criteria they decide on or the criteria decided on by the group. Space has been created for multiple observations in an attempt to support detailed observations and keep results organized.

Mini-Lesson 5.2

A Guide to Constructive Evaluation

Suggested Materials

- Student Design Notebooks (with completed copies of Handout 5.1)
- Student copies of Handout 5.2: A Guide to Constructive Evaluation

Sequence

1. Tell students that they are going to learn strategies for constructive evaluation. Point out that the word *constructive* comes from the word *construct*, meaning "to build." Constructive evaluation helps us build something new or better than we already have by showing us the materials or processes that contributed to us achieving our goal, as well as which ones could be replaced for better results.

2. Remind students that the prototype's job was to help them see what their ideas looked like when translated to the physical world. That means that everything they learned about their prototypes from testing is valuable information.

3. Distribute Handout 5.2: A Guide to Constructive Evaluation. As a class, read through the first two paragraphs of the handout.

4. Instruct each student/design team to complete the rest of Handout 5.2 following the instructions and using their completed Design Evaluation Data charts (Handout 5.1).

5. Discuss students' findings as a class. Suggested prompts for discussion include:
   o Which materials behaved as you expected?
   o Which materials behaved less effectively than you expected?
   o Which materials behaved more effectively than you expected?
   o What was the biggest surprise of the testing phase?
   o How did the shape and size of the prototypes affect their results?
   o What is the advantage of designing and building multiple prototypes?

CONCLUDING ACTIVITIES

Journal Prompts for Student Reflection

- What did you enjoy about testing your prototype?
- What did you find challenging about testing your prototype?
- How did your classmates help you? How did you help your classmates?
- How did it feel to evaluate your own prototype and the prototypes of others? Do you feel you were successful in offering constructive feedback? What are you most proud of?
- The next time you design and build a prototype, what would you like to do differently?
- Would anything have made the testing and evaluation process easier or more effective for you?
- What advice would you give to someone else who is about to build or test a prototype?

Suggested Assignments

- Thoughtfully respond to any three of the journal prompts in your Design Notebook.
- Write a paragraph expanding on your answer to the final question of Handout 5.2: A Guide to Constructive Evaluation.
- Write a letter to engineers explaining the prototype you would like them to build, based on your answer to the final question of Handout 5.2: A Guide to Constructive Evaluation. Be creative and include who you are, details about your organization, why you want the engineers to build the prototype, and what project it will be used for. You might use the letter you heard at the beginning of this unit, from Mariana T. Sandoval, as a model.
- Design the next prototype you would build, based on what you learned in the evaluation process. Create a work of art—a drawing, painting, collage, or graphic design—to represent this design.

Suggested Blog Posts

- A Beginner's Guide to Testing a Prototype
- Which Design Worked Better? A Side-by-Side Comparison of Three Prototypes
- The Top 10 Materials to Use for Underwater Design
- How to Learn from Your Mistakes When Building and Testing a Prototype
- 5 Tips for Ensuring a Successful Prototype Test

Name: _____ Date: _____

Handout 5.1

Design Evaluation Data

Directions: Add the evaluation criteria that you selected in class to the left-hand column of the table. As you test your prototype, write down the observations you make related to each criterion. If you have multiple observations about one criterion, or if you complete more than one timed test, use the Observation 2 and 3 columns.

Evaluation Criteria	Observation 1	Observation 2	Observation 3

COULD YOU LIVE UNDERWATER? © Taylor & Francis Group

Handout 5.2
A Guide to Constructive Evaluation

Directions: Remember, your prototype's job was to help you see what your idea looked like when it was translated to the physical world. That means that everything you learned about your prototype from testing it is valuable information.

Did things dissolve or break apart? What excellent intel! Did things stick together and behave as you expected? That's really useful to know! Were there complete surprises about the way materials behaved? Aren't you glad you know them now?

Use your Design Evaluation Data to answer the following questions.

1. Did the design remain in place? If it moved, how so?

2. How did the structure of your design hold up through testing?

3. How did the water affect your design?

Handout 5.2, Continued.

4. How long did you run your test? Did you observe a change over time?

5. Make a list of the design elements that you would use were you to build another prototype. Next to each element, note why you would include it and what role you would expect it to play.

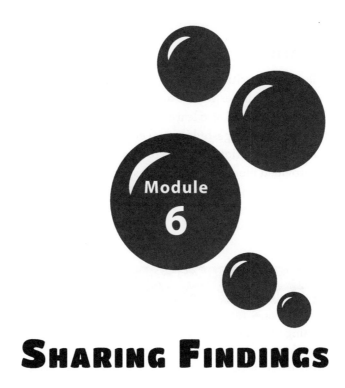

Module
6

Sharing Findings

Objectives

Students will learn the correct format for writing a formal business letter and will combine this activity with expository writing skills that help them summarize their experiences in this unit. Additionally, they will use their creativity to reflect on what they have learned and internalize their learning via their preferred modality.

Overview

In this module, students will reflect on their knowledge and organize their findings to share with their peers. The opportunity to return to the larger objective of the unit and see how they've addressed the problem presented to them offers students a chance to take pride in their work and see how much they've learned in the process of using design thinking.

Tech Connections

Students can create their final presentations via film, and can also film/photograph these presentations and share them on the classroom blog or social media pages. Using the hashtag #couldyouliveunderwater, they will be able to search for results from other classes and schools.

123   DOI: 10.4324/9781003233831-9

Writing Connections

Students will practice writing a formal business letter using the correct formatting and content. This letter will be an opportunity for them to summarize their work in this unit. They will also learn to create a table of contents by hand or on the computer. There are suggested journal entries and suggested blog posts in the Concluding Activities section. For classrooms keeping a blog, encourage students to use the provided blog post titles as inspiration for what they will write. Classes completing final projects will have additional opportunities to write. Refer to the one-week time frame.

Time Frame

Time Period	One Class Period (45–90 min.)	One Extended Period (90–120 min.)	One Week (5 Class Periods)
Activities	• Mini-Lesson 6.1: Writing a Response • Draft letters • Share letters with class • Mini-Lesson 6.2: Creating a Table of Contents • Compile and organize Design Notebooks	• Mini-Lesson 6.1: Writing a Response • Draft letters • Share letters with class • Mini-Lesson 6.2: Creating a Table of Contents • Compile and organize Design Notebooks • Create a visual to include with the letter	• Mini-Lesson 6.1: Writing a Response • Draft letters • Share letters with class • Mini-Lesson 6.2: Creating a Table of Contents • Compile and organize Design Notebooks • Create final projects • Present final projects • Concluding Activities

One Class Period: Students write a reply to the author of the letter they received in Module 1, describing what they learned during the process of researching, designing, building, and testing their prototype(s). They summarize their findings and make suggestions for the kind of design that would address the problem(s) they defined in Module 1. This letter becomes a summary and a record of what students learned, explored, and did in this unit. This activity can be completed as a class, with students contributing to a group brainstorm and outline to ensure the success for all students. Students compile their drawings, doodles, designs, and models—any planning materials they have generated—into their Design Notebook with a table of contents at the front. These notebooks can be displayed in the classroom.

One Extended Period: Students write a reply to the author of the letter they received in Module 1, describing what they learned during the process of researching, designing, building, and testing their prototype(s). They summarize their findings and make suggestions for the kind of design that would address the problem(s) they defined in Module 1. This letter becomes a summary and a record of what students learned, explored, and did in this unit.

Students create visuals—drawings, computer designs, or collages—of their proposed design to include with their letters. Students compile their drawings, doodles, designs, and models—any planning materials they have generated—into their Design Notebook with a table of contents at the front. These notebooks can be displayed in the classroom.

One Week: Students write a reply to the author of the letter they received in Module 1, describing what they learned during the process of researching, designing, building, and testing their prototype(s). They summarize their findings and make suggestions for the kind of design that would address the problem(s) they defined in Module 1. This letter becomes a summary and a record of what students learned, explored, and did in this unit.

Students compile their drawings, doodles, designs, and models—any planning materials they have generated—into their Design Notebook with a table of contents at the front. Students will also work in groups or individually to create multimedia presentations of their design, prototype, test, and modification stages. Possible ideas for presentations include:

- a video describing the project and all its stages (students may want to invent characters and make this an imaginative process);
- a series of blog posts to be posted on the classroom or school blog/website;
- a lesson the students teach to the rest of the class about how to successfully use design thinking for a project (students may want to invent characters and make this an imaginative process);
- a mural or collage illustrating the design thinking process and all its stages;
- reenactments of stages of the design thinking process, done live or recorded (students may want to invent characters and make this an imaginative process); or
- choosing one key idea, such as "resilience," "cooperation," "flexibility," or "curiosity," and tracing how that idea was part of each stage of the design thinking process.

Both the presentations and the notebooks can be displayed in the classroom.
- **Day 1:** Students draft their letters and plan their presentations.
- **Day 2:** Students create their presentations.
- **Day 3:** Students continue creating their presentations.
- **Day 4:** Students continue creating their presentations.
- **Day 5:** Students share their presentations. Students complete Concluding Activities.

WRITING A RESPONSE

Suggested Materials

- Student Design Notebooks (with Handout 1.9 accessible)
- Handout 6.1: Business Letter Template
- Handout 6.2: Letter Outline

Sequence

1. Tell students they will be writing a response letter to Mariana T. Sandoval, whose letter they read or heard in Module 1.
2. Distribute Handout 6.1: Business Letter Template, and walk students through the structure of a business letter. Invite questions and discussion about how a business letter is different from a personal letter.
3. Distribute Handout 6.2: Letter Outline. Ask students to begin planning their letters using the outline while you circulate to answer questions and offer support.
4. Instruct students to draft their letters.
5. If time allows, students can switch papers and utilize peer editing, using Handout 1.9: What Should I Say?: A Guide to Effective Feedback.
6. Have students proofread their letters.

Mini-Lesson 6.2

CREATING A TABLE OF CONTENTS

Suggested Materials

- Student Design Notebooks
- Any material not yet in student Design Notebooks

Sequence

1. Ask a few students to select nonfiction or reference books off of the shelves of the classroom and open up to the table of contents. Discuss the purpose of this feature and ask students why it's useful.

2. Next, discuss the organization of the tables of contents. Do they show larger and smaller views of the material, such as units, chapters, and sections? How do they indicate the hierarchy of ideas? Is it through indentation? Color? Typeface?

3. Tell students that they will be creating tables of contents for their own Design Notebooks. They will need to think through the organization system they want to use. Invite them to use the design thinking process posters from the beginning of the unit as a guide, and also to use their own best judgment of how the material should be presented.

4. Some students may want to design the table of contents first, writing or typing it out and then using it as a guide to put the material in order and adding page numbers last. Other students may feel more comfortable physically organizing the material first, adding page numbers to the ordered material, and then creating the table of contents last. Invite students to take charge of how they organize this process, possibly working together in order to bounce ideas off of one another.

CONCLUDING ACTIVITIES

Journal Prompts for Student Reflection

- What are some other real-world problems that you can imagine being solved by design thinking? Which one would you be interested in helping to solve?
- Which stage of design thinking was the most challenging for you? Which stage of design thinking was the most fun for you?
- How did working with your classmates and your teacher impact you during this unit? Were you able to collaborate? Was it hard to compromise? Do you think design thinking is easier to do alone or with other people? Why?
- Why do you think the final stage of this project was sharing your work?
- If the underwater habitats were ready for families to move into, would you want to move into one? Why or why not? What do you think the experience would be like?
- What advice would you give to someone else who is about to engage in a design thinking project?

Suggested Assignments

- Thoughtfully respond to any three of the journal prompts.
- Film or photograph your Design Notebook to be shared on the classroom blog or via social media, using the hashtag #couldyouliveunderwater.

Suggested Blog Posts

- The Top 10 Things I Learned from Using Design Thinking
- The 5 Stages of Design Thinking
- A Beginner's Guide to Design Thinking
- The Pros and Cons of Collaborating with Classmates

Handout 6.1

Business Letter Template

Directions: You will be writing a response letter to Mariana T. Sandoval. This will need to be a business letter. A business letter is different from a personal letter. Take a look at the format below.

Sender's Name
Street Address
City, State Zip Code

Date

Name of Recipient
Title of Recipient
Street Address
City, State Zip Code

Dear [Name of Recipient]:
Introductory Paragraph
Body Paragraphs
Concluding Paragraph

Sincerely,
[Your Name]

COULD YOU LIVE UNDERWATER? © Taylor & Francis Group

Handout 6.2

Letter Outline

Directions: Use this outline to plan your response letter to Mariana T. Sandoval. Once you have taken notes, draft your letter by turning your notes from each section into complete sentences.

1. **Introductory Paragraph:**
   a. Introduce yourself.

   b. State the intention of the letter. (Hint: Look at the body paragraphs.)

2. **Body Paragraph 1: Describe Module 1:**
   a. What did you do?

   b. What did you learn?

   c. What recommendations do you have for others completing similar tasks?

Handout 6.2, Continued.

3. **Body Paragraph 2: Describe Module 2:**
   a. What did you do?

   b. What did you learn?

   c. What recommendations do you have for others completing similar tasks?

4. **Body Paragraph 3: Describe Module 3:**
   a. What did you do?

   b. What did you learn?

   c. What recommendations do you have for others completing similar tasks?

Handout 6.2, Continued.

5. **Body Paragraph 4: Describe Module 4:**
   a. What did you do?

   b. What did you learn?

   c. What recommendations do you have for others completing similar tasks?

6. **Body Paragraph 5: Describe Module 5:**
   a. What did you do?

   b. What did you learn?

   c. What recommendations do you have for others completing similar tasks?

Handout 6.2, Continued.

7. **Body Paragraph 6: Describe Module 6:**
   a. What did you do?

   b. What did you learn?

   c. What recommendations do you have for others completing similar tasks?

8. **Concluding Paragraph:**
   a. How do you feel about this experience overall?

   b. What do you hope to do next with your design thinking knowledge?

Appendix A
Design Thinking
Resources

IDEO
Design Thinking Resources
https://www.ideou.com/pages/design-thinking-resources

Stanford's d.school
A Virtual Crash Course in Design Thinking
https://dschool.stanford.edu/resources-collections/a-virtal-crash-course-in-design-thinking

***Launch: Using Design Thinking to Boost Creativity and Bring out the Maker in Every Student* by John Spencer and A.J. Juliani**
http://thelaunchcycle.com

APPENDIX B
RESOURCES FOR CREATING
A CLASSROOM BLOG

Free platforms for your classroom blog include:
- Blogger: https://www.blogger.com
- Medium: https://medium.com
- Tumblr: https://www.tumblr.com
- Weebly: https://www.weebly.com
- Wix: https://www.wix.com
- WordPress: https://wordpress.com
- Yola: https://www.yola.com

Sources for licensing free or inexpensive stock photos for blog posts include:
- 123RF: https://www.123rf.com
- Canva: https://www.canva.com

Teacher's Note. Canva is a free, online photo-editing site. It has templates for creating images for various purposes, including Twitter headers, social media posts, and blog headers. It also has an image library containing photographs and illustrations. Many images are free to use, and others may be licensed for $1.00. Designs can be saved to your account and duplicated, making it easy to create custom featured images with a consistent look for blog posts.

APPENDIX C
RUBRICS

Name: _____   Date: _____

Writing Assessment Rubric

Assignment: _____

	0 points	10 points	20 points
Logical Organization	Necessary structural elements, such as topic and concluding sentences, are missing. Presentation of ideas is incoherent.	Some structural elements, such as topic and concluding sentences, are present. Presentation of ideas is somewhat coherent.	All structural elements, such as topic and concluding sentences, are present. Presentation of ideas is coherent and engaging.
Relevant Content	Content is off-topic. Purpose of writing is not addressed. Audience is not taken into consideration.	Content is somewhat on-topic. Purpose of writing is addressed, but it may be done clumsily. Audience is taken into account in a limited way.	Content is on-topic. Purpose of writing is addressed clearly. Audience is taken into account, as evidenced by tone and length of writing.
Style and Flow	Does not make use of expected transitions, range of vocabulary, or sentence structure or sentence-type variety.	Makes some use of expected transitions, range of vocabulary, and sentence structure or sentence-type variety.	Consistently makes use of expected transitions, range of vocabulary, and sentence structure or sentence-type variety.
Grammar and Conventions	Includes an overwhelming number of errors in spelling, grammar, usage, and punctuation that could have been avoided with proper proofreading. Errors prevent understanding.	Includes a moderate number of errors in spelling grammar, usage, and punctuation. Proofreading is evident but not careful. Errors may affect reader's understanding.	Includes very few to no errors in spelling, grammar, usage, and punctuation. Careful proofreading is evident. Errors do not affect reader's understanding.
Appearance	Penmanship is very sloppy or illegible. The writing has not been formatted at all.	Penmanship is legible but not the student's best effort. The writing is partially formatted correctly but has many errors.	Penmanship is the student's best effort. The writing is correctly formatted.

Hands-On Activity Assessment Rubric

Assignment: _____

	0 points	10 points	20 points
Work With Purpose	Student does not develop a plan or work to execute it.	Student develops some plan but becomes distracted or does not follow through.	Student develops a plan and follows through with it.
Demonstrates Flexible Thinking	Student is not open to the ideas of others.	Student is open to the ideas of others when his or her own ideas don't work.	Student looks forward to the next challenge and sees feedback as supporting his or her learning and grows from it.
Kindness and Collaboration	Student is consistently disrespectful and unkind to others, does not listen to others or share ideas, and struggles to resolve differences.	Student is somewhat respectful and kind to others, demonstrates inconsistent proficiency at listening and sharing ideas, and sometimes resolves differences with respect.	Student is consistently respectful and kind to others, demonstrates excellence at listening and sharing ideas, and consistently resolves differences with respect.
Enthusiasm	Student rarely or never finds joy in learning and creating. Student does not bring new ideas or perspectives to the project.	Student sometimes finds joy in learning and creating. Student sometimes brings new ideas and perspectives to the project.	Student consistently finds joy in learning and creating. Student brings new ideas and perspectives to whatever he or she is working on and asks questions to deepen his or her understanding.
Respect for People and Materials	Student is not mindful of others, the space, or the materials, taking more than is needed or wasting materials. Student does not respond to people when they say "No" or "Stop."	Student is somewhat mindful of others, the space, and the materials, but may take more than is needed. Student sometimes asks before touching another person or another person's belongings, projects, etc. Student must be asked multiple times to stop when others say "No" or "Stop."	Student is mindful of others, the space, and the materials, only taking what he or she needs. Student asks before touching another person or another person's belongings, projects, etc. Student responds immediately to people when they say "No" or "Stop."

Design Notebook
Assessment Rubric

	0 points	10 points	20 points
Logical Organization	Table of contents is missing. Materials are in random order.	Table of contents may have some errors. Materials are somewhat organized.	Table of contents is clear and accurate. Materials are organized according to the stages of design thinking.
Completeness	Includes very few or no materials from the unit.	Includes at least half of the materials from the unit.	All materials from the unit are included.
Includes Student's Notes	Includes no student notes.	Includes some student notes.	Includes copious student notes, indicating creative ownership of the project.
Writing and Grammar	Includes little to no writing. Errors prevent understanding.	Writing was not proofread and revised. Many words are spelled incorrectly. Errors may affect reader's understanding.	The writing has been proofread and revised. Few errors. Errors do not affect reader's understanding.
Appearance	It appears that no effort was made to create an attractive, engaging notebook.	Some effort was made to create an attractive, engaging notebook.	The notebook is attractive and engaging.

ABOUT THE AUTHORS

Megan Barnhard is an author, writing coach, and curriculum creator committed to helping writers tame the writing process and enjoy self-expression. She lives on the Central Coast of California with her hilarious husband and her cat, Bradbury.

Jade Rivera is a micro-school builder, author, and STEM educator dedicated to helping gifted learners thrive. She lives in Oakland, CA, with her wonderful husband and her two cats, Rose and Joey.

COMMON CORE STATE STANDARDS ALIGNMENT

Grade Level	Common Core State Standards
Grade 4 ELA-Literacy	W.4.2 Write informative/explanatory texts to examine a topic and convey ideas and information clearly.
	W.4.4 Produce clear and coherent writing in which the development and organization are appropriate to task, purpose, and audience.
	W.4.5 With guidance and support from peers and adults, develop and strengthen writing as needed by planning, revising, and editing.
	W.4.6 With some guidance and support from adults, use technology, including the Internet, to produce and publish writing as well as to interact and collaborate with others; demonstrate sufficient command of keyboarding skills to type a minimum of one page in a single sitting.
	W.4.7 Conduct short research projects that build knowledge through investigation of different aspects of a topic.
	W.4.8 Recall relevant information from experiences or gather relevant information from print and digital sources; take notes and categorize information, and provide a list of sources.
	W.4.9 Draw evidence from literary or informational texts to support analysis, reflection, and research.
Grade 5 ELA-Literacy	W.5.2 Write informative/explanatory texts to examine a topic and convey ideas and information clearly.
	W.5.4 Produce clear and coherent writing in which the development and organization are appropriate to task, purpose, and audience.
	W.5.5 With guidance and support from peers and adults, develop and strengthen writing as needed by planning, revising, editing, rewriting, or trying a new approach.

Grade Level	Common Core State Standards
Grade 5 ELA-Literacy, *continued.*	W.5.6 With some guidance and support from adults, use technology, including the Internet, to produce and publish writing as well as to interact and collaborate with others; demonstrate sufficient command of keyboarding skills to type a minimum of two pages in a single sitting.
	W.5.7 Conduct short research projects that use several sources to build knowledge through investigation of different aspects of a topic.
	W.5.8 Recall relevant information from experiences or gather relevant information from print and digital sources; summarize or paraphrase information in notes and finished work, and provide a list of sources.
	W.5.9 Draw evidence from literary or informational texts to support analysis, reflection, and research.

NEXT GENERATION SCIENCE STANDARDS ALIGNMENT

Grade Level	Next Generation Science Standards
Grades 3–5	3-5-ETS1-1. Define a simple design problem reflecting a need or a want that includes specified criteria for success and constraints on materials, time, or cost.
	3-5-ETS1-2. Generate and compare multiple possible solutions to a problem based on how well each is likely to meet the criteria and constraints of the problem.
	3-5-ETS1-3. Plan and carry out fair tests in which variables are controlled and failure points are considered to identify aspects of a model or prototype that can be improved.

*For Product Safety Concerns and Information please contact
our EU representative GPSR@taylorandfrancis.com Taylor & Francis
Verlag GmbH, Kaufingerstraße 24, 80331 München, Germany*

T - #0075 - 090625 - C0 - 279/216/9 - PB - 9781618217509 - Gloss Lamination